Rebrand 1969

Rebrand 1969

National Gallery of Art

SMITHSONIAN INSTITUTION

BOOK OF ILLUSTRATIONS

WASHINGTON, D. C.

First Edition _____March, 1941

Second Printing _____April, 1941

Second Edition _____April, 1942

Foreword

This volume contains reproductions of paintings and sculpture in the permanent collection of the National Gallery and certain loans from the Kress Collection which have been on exhibition since the Gallery was first opened. The reproductions are arranged according to national schools. Within each school the order of arrangement is alphabetical, according to the name of the artist. A complete list of works reproduced, in the order of their catalogue numbers, appears at the end of the volume. This list indicates, besides artist and title, the donor of each work of art.

TABLE OF CONTENTS

	PAGE
American School	5
British Schools	11
Dutch Schools	21
Flemish and German Schools	35
French School	43
Italian Schools	49
Spanish Schools	209
Sculpture — French School	217
Sculpture — Italian Schools	221
List of Paintings	239
List of Sculpture	253

AMERICAN SCHOOL

487   BROWN, MATHER   William Vans Murray   497   COPLEY   Richard, Earl Howe

493   HARDING, CHESTER   John Randolph

488   SAVAGE   The Washington Family

489   STUART   Joseph Coolidge   491   STUART   Lawrence Yates

George Washington

495   STUART   John Randolph

490   STUART   Mrs. Richard Yates

494   TRUMBULL   Alexander Hamilton

496   WEST, BENJAMIN   Colonel Guy Johnson

BRITISH SCHOOLS

108 CONSTABLE A View of Salisbury Cathedral

100 GAINSBOROUGH Mrs. John Taylor 99 GAINSBOROUGH Miss Catherine Tatton

93   GAINSBOROUGH   Georgiana,
Duchess of Devonshire

98   GAINSBOROUGH   George IV as Prince of Wales

107   GAINSBOROUGH   Landscape with a Bridge

92 GAINSBOROUGH Mrs. Richard Brinsley Sheridan

111   HOPPNER   The Frankland Sisters   96   LAWRENCE   Lady Templeton and Her Son

101   RAEBURN   Miss Eleanor Urquhart

103 RAEBURN John Tait and His Grandson

102 RAEBURN Colonel Francis James Scott

97 REYNOLDS Lady Elizabeth Compton

95 REYNOLDS Lady Elizabeth Delmé and Her Children

106   REYNOLDS   Lady Caroline Howard   94   ROMNEY   Lady Broughton

104   ROMNEY   Miss Willoughby   105   ROMNEY   Mrs. Davenport

109   TURNER   Mortlake Terrace

110   TURNER   Approach to Venice

DUTCH SCHOOLS

59   CUYP   Herdsmen Tending Cattle

501   CUYP   The Maas at Dordrecht

69   HALS, FRANS   Balthasar Coymans

68   HALS, FRANS   Portrait of an Officer

71   HALS, FRANS   Portrait of a Young Man

70   HALS, FRANS   Portrait of a Man

67   HALS, FRANS   Portrait of an Elderly Lady

498   HALS, FRANS   A Young Man in a Large Hat

60   HOBBEMA   A Farm in the Sunlight

61   HOBBEMA   A Wooded Landscape

62   HOBBEMA   A View on a High Road

56   de HOOCH   A Dutch Courtyard

63   MAES   An Old Woman Dozing Over a Book   52   MOR   Portrait of a Gentleman

57   METSU   The Intruder

Self-Portrait

74   REMBRANDT   A Girl with a Broom

73   REMBRANDT   An Old Lady with a Book

75   REMBRANDT   A Woman Holding a Pink

76   REMBRANDT   Lucretia

78 REMBRANDT A Polish Nobleman

77 REMBRANDT A Young Man Seated at a Table

79 REMBRANDT Joseph Accused by Potiphar's Wife

499 REMBRANDT A Turk

58   TER BORCH   The Suitor's Visit

53   VERMEER   The Girl with a Red Hat

54   VERMEER   The Lacemaker

55   VERMEER   The Smiling Girl

FLEMISH AND GERMAN
SCHOOLS

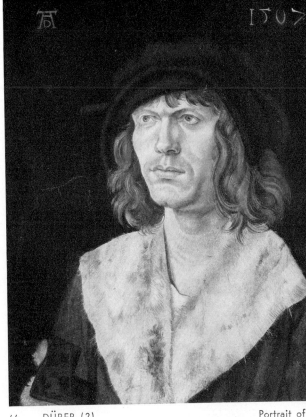

40   CHRISTUS, PETRUS   The Nativity   66   DÜRER (?)   Portrait of a Man

43   DAVID, GERARD   The Rest on the Flight into Egypt

64   HOLBEIN, THE YOUNGER   Edward VI
                                            as Prince of Wales

39   van EYCK, JAN   The Annunciation

65   HOLBEIN, THE YOUNGER   Sir Brian Tuke

41   MEMLING Madonna and Child with Angels   42   MEMLING Portrait of a Man with an Arrow

47   RUBENS   Isabella Brant

46   SITHIUM, MIGUEL   A Knight of the Order of Calatrava

48   VAN DYCK   Susanna Fourment and Her Daughter

50   VAN DYCK   Philip, Lord Wharton

51   VAN DYCK   William II of Nassau and Orange

49 VAN DYCK

Marchesa Balbi

500   VAN DYCK   Portrait of a Flemish Lady

45   van der WEYDEN   Christ Appearing
                                            to the Virgin

44   van der WEYDEN   Portrait of a Lady

FRENCH SCHOOL

The House of Cards

91   CHARDIN   The Young Governess

545   DAUMIER   Advice to a Young Artist

89 LANCRET   La Camargo Dancing

ITALIAN SCHOOLS

176 ALBERTINELLI and FRA BARTOLOMMEO — Madonna and Child with Saints and Angels

485 ALBERTINELLI — Madonna and Child

170 ALLORI, ALESSANDRO — Portrait of a Boy in Red

318 ALUNNO DI BENOZZO — Processional Cross

159   ALLORI, ALESSANDRO

Portrait of a Youth

152   ANDREA DI BARTOLO   The Presentation in the Temple   153   ANDREA DI BARTOLO   The Nativity of the Virgin

154   ANDREA DI BARTOLO   Joachim and the Beggars

241   ANDREA DA FIRENZE
The Crucifixion

223   ANDREA DI GIUSTO   The Assumption of the Virgin

246   ANDREA DI GIUSTO   A Judgment Scene

449   ANDREA DEL SARTO   Madonna and Child with the Infant St. John

371   ANGELICO, FRA   The Entombment

5 ANGELICO, FRA The Madonna of Humility

256 ANGELICO, FRA The Meeting of St. Francis and St. Dominic

30 ANTONELLO DA MESSINA Madonna and Child

31 ANTONELLO DA MESSINA Portrait of a Young Man

315   ANTONELLO DA SALIBA   Abraham Visited by the Angels

144   ANTONELLO DA SALIBA   Madonna and Child
                                        with the Infant St. John

280   ANTONIAZZO ROMANO   The Crucifixion with St. Francis

348 ANTONIO VENEZIANO   St. Paul

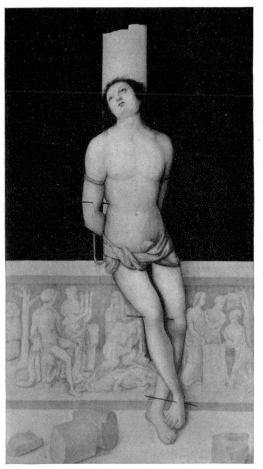

414   ASPERTINI   St. Sebastian

312 ANTONIO DA VITERBO   Pietà

272   BACCHIACCA   Allegory

325   BALDOVINETTI   Madonna and Child

217   BALDUCCI   Venus and Cupid

427   BANCHI   Madonna and Child

412   BARNABA DA MODENA   The Crucifixion

388
BARNABA
DA MODENA

Madonna and
Child

276   BAROCCIO   Quintilia Fischieri   242   BARONZIO   The Baptism of Chris

452   BARONZIO   The Adoration of the Magi

467   BARTOLOMMEO, FRA   The Creation of Eve

470   BARTOLOMMEO, FRA and   The Holy Family with Saints
       FRA PAOLINO

151   BARTOLOMMEO DI GIOVANNI   A King with His
                                   Counsellors

150   BARTOLOMMEO DI GIOVANNI   A Tribute to Apollo

313   BARTOLOMMEO DI GIOVANNI   The Adoration of the Magi

368   BARTOLOMMEO VENETO   Portrait of a Gentleman

255   BASAITI   Madonna Adoring the Child

287   BASAITI   Madonna and Child   237   BASSANO, JACOPO   The Annunciation to the Shepherds

275   BAZZANI   The Prodigal Son (?)

301   BAZZANI   A Laughing Man

529   BECCAFUMI   The Holy Family with Angels

28   BELLINI, GIOVANNI   The Flight into Egypt

29   BELLINI, GIOVANNI   Portrait of a Young Man in Red   293   BELLINI, GIOVANNI   Portrait of a Young Man

316   BELLINI, GIOVANNI ·   Portrait of a Man

328   BELLINI, GIOVANNI   St. Jerome Reading

335   BELLINI, GIOVANNI   Portrait of a Condottiere

365   BELLINI, GIOVANNI   Portrait of a Venetian Gentleman   373   BELLINI, GIOVANNI   Madonna and Child in a Landscape

448   BELLINI, GIOVANNI   Portrait of a Senator

445   BELLINI, GIOVANNI   Madonna and Child

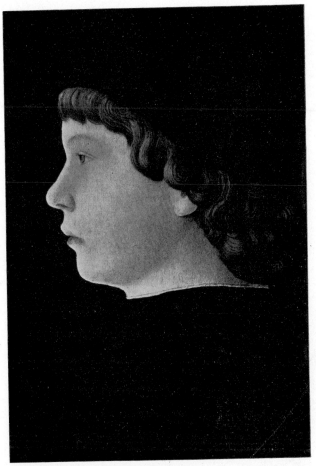

538   BELLINI, GIOVANNI   Madonna and Child   374   BELLINI, JACOPO   Profile Portrait of a Boy
                                  with Saints

509   BELLINI, JACOPO (?)   Christ Washing the Feet of the Apostles

128   BEMBO, BENEDETTO   St. John Preaching

10   BENVENUTO DI GIOVANNI   The Adoration of the Magi

429   BENVENUTO DI GIOVANNI   The Agony in the Garden

119   BOCCACCINO,   St. John the Evangelist   120   BOCCACCINO,   St. Matthew
      PSEUDO-   PSEUDO-

512   BOCCACCINO, PSEUDO-   The Adoration of the Shepherds   308   BOCCATI   Portrait of a Monk

421   BOCCATI   Madonna and Child   518   BOCCATI   St. John the Baptist
                                                                                        and St. Sebastian

524   BOLTRAFFIO   Madonna and Child

206   BONIFAZIO VERONESE   The Crowning of St. Catherine of Alexandria

171   BORDONE   Diana

474   BORDONE   Minerva at the Forge of Vulcan   436   BORGOGNONE   Madonna and Child

19   BOTTICELLI   Portrait of a Youth   21   BOTTICELLI   Madonna and Child

22   BOTTICELLI   The Adoration of the Magi

535 BOTTICELLI   Madonna and Child

112   BOTTICELLI   Crucifix   295   BRAMANTINO   Madonna and Child

142   BUGIARDINI   Portrait of a Young Woman   I   BYZANTINE SCHOOL   Enthroned Madonna
                                                                                                                and Child

234   CANALETTO   A View of the Ducal Palace, Venice

270   CARAVAGGIO   Still Life

419   CARIANI   Portrait of a Gentleman

478   CAROTO   The Entombment

133   CARPACCIO, VITTORE   Temperance

129   CARPACCIO, VITTORE   Prudence

227   CARPACCIO, VITTORE   Madonna and Child with Two Saints

260   CARPACCIO, VITTORE   261   CARPACCIO, VITTORE   304   CARPACCIO, VITTORE   305   CARPACCIO, VITTORE
St. Nicholas (?)   St. Peter Martyr   St. Stephen   St. John the Baptist

447   CARPACCIO, VITTORE   A Saint Reading

177   CARRIERA, ROSALBA   Sir John Reade, Bart.

247   CARRIERA, ROSALBA   Allegory of Painting

307   CATENA   Portrait of a Man

155   CATENA   Portrait of a Woman

433   CATENA   Christ and the Samaritan Woman   245   CENNI DI FRANCESCO   Madonna
                                                                                                    and Child

33   CIMA   Madonna and Child with St. Jerome and St. John the Baptist

279   CIMA   St. Jerome in the Wilderness

288   CIMABUE (?)   The Capture of Christ in the Garden

2   CIMABUE   Christ between St. Peter and St. James Major

311   CIMABUE (?)   The Last Supper

477   CIVERCHIO   St. Peter

527   CIMABUE, CONTEMPORARY OF   Madonna and Child with Saints

194   CORREGGIO   The Mystic Marriage of St. Catherine

346   CORREGGIO   Portrait of a Young Girl

356   CORREGGIO (?)   Madonna and Child

226   COSSA   Madonna and Child with Angels

338   COSSA   St. Liberal

339   COSSA   St. Lucy

| 281 | COSTA | St. Nicholas of Tolentino and St. Christopher | 282 | COSTA | St. Julianus and St. Vincent |
| 283 | COSTA | St. Catherine and St. Roch | 284 | COSTA | St. Sebastian and St. Lucy |

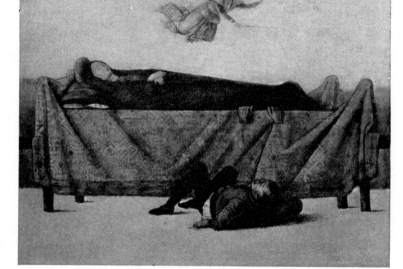

364   COSTA   St. Paul   395   COSTA   The Miracle of the Catafalque

397   COSTA   The Miracle of the Catafalque

396   COSTA   The Miracle of the Catafalque

187   COZZARELLI   Madonna and Child with Angels   507   COZZARELLI   Scenes from the Life of the Virgin

173   CRESPI, G. M.   Cupids with Sleeping Nymphs

530   CRESPI, G. M.   Portrait of a Girl

147   CRIVELLI, CARLO   148   CRIVELLI, CARLO
              St. Francis   St. Nicodemus (?)

320   CRIVELLI, VITTORE   St. Francis

375   CRIVELLI, CARLO   Madonna and Child

195   DADDI   The Flagellation

196   DADDI   St. Catherine

457   DADDI   Madonna and Child
                                Enthroned with Saints

511   DADDI   Madonna and Child
                                          with Donor

519   DADDI   Madonna and Child
                          Enthroned with Saints and Angels

200   DADDI, FOLLOWER OF   Madonna and Child with Saints

354   DIAMANTE, FRA   355   DIAMANTE, FRA   398   DIAMANTE, FRA
       Two Saints   Two Saints   Two Saints

249   DIANA   Madonna and Child with St. Jerome

424   DOMENICO DI MICHELINO   The Seven Arts

425   DOMENICO DI MICHELINO   The Seven Virtues

15   DOMENICO VENEZIANO   Matteo Olivieri

332   DOMENICO VENEZIANO   Madonna and Child

251   DOMENICO VENEZIANO   St. Francis Receiving
                                      the Stigmata

526   DOMENICO VENEZIANO (?)
                                 St. John the Baptist

209   DOSSO DOSSI   The Standard Bearer   481   DOSSO DOSSI   St. Lucretia

361   DOSSO DOSSI   Scene from a Legend

8   DUCCIO   Nativity with the Prophets Isaiah and Ezekiel

252   DUCCIO   The Calling of the Apostles Peter and Andrew

510   DUCCIO, CONTEMPORARY OF   Madonna and Child with Saints and the Crucifixion

137   FEI, PAOLO DI GIOVANNI   Christ on the Road to Calvary

193   FEI, PAOLO DI GIOVANNI   Madonna and Child
                                          between Two Angels,
                                       St. Francis and St. Louis

199   FETI   The Parable of Dives and Lazarus

232   FLORENTINE SCHOOL,   Madonna and Child
       XV CENTURY   with Angels

248   FLORENTINE SCHOOL, XV CENTURY   Scenes from a Legend

169   FLORENTINE SCHOOL, XVI CENTURY   A Scene from the Life of St. Nicholas

443   FLORENTINE SCHOOL, XVI CENTURY   Apollo and Marsyas

386   FOPPA   St. Christopher

460   FOPPA   Madonna and Child

353   FRANCESCO DI GIORGIO   The Visit of Cleopatra to Antony

415   FRANCESCO DI GIORGIO   The Meeting of Dido and Aeneas

· BENEDICTA TV IN MVLIERIBVS ET BENEDICTVS FRVCTVS VENTRIS TVI

306   FRANCIA   Madonna and Child with the Infant St. John

184   FRANCIA   Madonna and Child

210   FRANCIABIGIO   Portrait of a Young Man

472   FRANCIABIGIO   Madonna and Child

321   FUNGAI   St. Louis
of France

230   FUNGAI   The Martyrdom of St. Lucy

4   GADDI, AGNOLO   Madonna Enthroned with Saints and Angels

239   GADDI, AGNOLO   Madonna
and Child with Saints and Angels

314   GADDI, AGNOLO   The Coronation
of the Virgin

181   GADDI, AGNOLO   The Annunciation with Donor

473   GAROFALO   The Meditation of St. Jerome

212   GAROFALO   The Baptism of Christ   216   GAUDENZIO FERRARI   The Adoration
                                                                                          of the Child

167 GENGA — St. Augustine and the Three Catechumens

420 GENTILE DA FABRIANO — Madonna and Child with Two Angels

379 GENTILE DA FABRIANO — A Miracle of St. Nicholas

366   GENTILE DA FABRIANO   Madonna and Child

381 GHIRLANDAIO, DOMENICO   St. Michael

380 GHIRLANDAIO, DOMENICO   St. Dominic

113 GHIRLANDAIO, RIDOLFO   Taddeo Taddei

213 GHISLANDI   Portrait of a Young Man

191   GIAMBONO   St. Peter

418   GIANNICOLA DI PAOLO   The Crucifixion with
the Four Holy Women

440   GIAMPIETRINO   Portrait of a Lady as the Magdalen

400   GIORGIONE   The Adoration of the Shepherds

369   GIORGIONE and TITIAN   Portrait of a Venetian Gentleman

253   GIORGIONE (?)   Venus and Cupid in a Landscape

367   GIOTTO   Madonna and Child

3   GIOTTO, FOLLOWER OF   St. Paul

423   GIOTTO, FOLLOWER OF   The Crucifixion

486   GIOVANNI DEL BIONDO   The Annunciation

238   GIOVANNI DEL BIONDO   Madonna and Child, St. John   347   GIOVANNI DA BOLOGNA
                                  the Baptist, and St. Catherine   The Coronation of the Virgin

197   GIOVANNI DA MILANO   St. Anthony   116   GIOVANNI DI NICCOLÒ DA PISA
                                      Abbot   Madonna and Child with Angels

13   GIOVANNI DI PAOLO   The Adoration of the Magi

334   GIOVANNI DI PAOLO   The Annunciation

351   GIOVANNI DI PAOLO   Madonna and Child
                                                    with Saints and Angels

462   GIOVANNI DI PAOLO   St. Luke the Evangelist

393   GIOVANNI DI PAOLO   The Assumption of the Virgin

265   GIOVANNI DAL PONTE   Madonna and Child with Saints

446   GIROLAMO DI BENVENUTO   Portrait of a Young Woman   508   GIROLAMO DI BENVENUTO   The Nativity
                                                                                                with St. Jerome

475   GIROLAMO DA CARPI   The Assumption of the Virgin

484   GIROLAMO DA TREVISO   Madonna and Child

192   GIUSTO DE' MENABUOI   St. Paul and
                                 St. Augustine

376   GOZZOLI   St. Ursula with
                                              Angels and Donor

437   GRANACCI   Scenes from a Legend

417   GRANACCI   The Holy Family   515   GRANACCI   Madonna and Child with Two Angels

168   GUALTIERI DI GIOVANNI   Madonna and Child

224   GUARDI   View on the Cannareggio, Venice

292   GUARDI   The Holy Family with St. Catherine

240   GUARDI   Campo San Zanipolo

459   GUARIENTO   Madonna and Child
                                                         with Four Saints

466   INGANNATI   St. Catherine

520   ITALIAN SCHOOL (CENTRAL)
       XIII CENTURY
              Madonna and Child with Angels

516   JACOPO DEL CASENTINO   St. John the Baptist   517   JACOPO DEL CASENTINO   St. Lucy

359   JACOPO DEL CASENTINO   The Presentation   149   JACOPO DI CIONE
                                   in the Temple   Madonna and Child with Saints

262   JACOPO DI CIONE   The Dead Christ with Madonna, St. John, and Donor

286   LATTANZIO DA RIMINI   Madonna and Child in a Landscape

205   LICINIO   Portrait of a Musician

208   LIPPI, FILIPPINO, AND ASSISTANTS   St. Francis in Glory

298   LIPPI, FILIPPINO   St. Donatus

299   LIPPI, FILIPPINO   St. Augustine

340   LIPPI, FILIPPINO   Tobias and the Angel

537   LIPPI, FILIPPINO   The Coronation of the Virgin

18   LIPPI, FILIPPINO   Madonna Adoring the Child,   20   LIPPI, FILIPPINO   Portrait of a Youth
                                              with an Angel

401   LIPPI, FRA FILIPPO   Madonna and Child

536   LIPPI, FRA FILIPPO   The Annunciation

390   LIPPI, FRA FILIPPO   The Nativity

407   LIPPI, FRA FILIPPO   Head of the Madonna

130   LOMBARD SCHOOL, XV CENTURY
                   Madonna and Child with Saints and Donor

174   LONGHI, PIETRO   The Simulated Faint

175   LONGHI, PIETRO   Blind Man's Buff

250   LORENZETTI, PIETRO   Madonna and Child with Saints

360   LORENZETTI, PIETRO   St. Clare

546 LORENZETTI, PIETRO   Madonna and Child with St. Mary Magdalen and St. Catherine

521   LORENZETTI, PIETRO   St. Catherine
of Alexandria

134 LORENZETTI, PIETRO,   The
FOLLOWER OF   Crucifixion

441   LORENZETTI, UGOLINO   The
                                   Crucifixion

164   LORENZETTI,   St. Mary
       UGOLINO   Magdalen

514   LORENZO MONACO   Madonna
                              and Child

461 LORENZO DI NICCOLÒ   The Crucifixion
with Madonna and Saints

411 LORENZO VENEZIANO   Madonna and Child

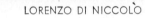

207 LOTTO   Portrait of a Man

228 LOTTO   St. Catherine

258   LOTTO   A Maiden's Dream

267   LOTTO   Allegory

399   LOTTO   The Nativity

453   LUCA DI TOMMÈ   Madonna and Child
                                          with Angels

136   LUCA DI TOMMÈ   The Crucifixion

231   LUINI   Venus

455   LUINI   The Nativity

37   LUINI   Portrait of a Lady

263   LUINI   The Madonna of the Carnation   482   MAGNASCO   Seascape with Friars

528   MAGNASCO   The Baptism of Christ

532   MAGNASCO   Christ Calling St. Peter

476   MAGNASCO   Landscape with Figures

523   MAINERI   Ex Voto

244   MAINARDI   Madonna and Child with St. John and Angels

32   MANTEGNA   St. Jerome in the Wilderness   289   MANTEGNA   Judith with the
                                                                                                      Head of Holofernes

377 MANTEGNA   Madonna and Child

121   MANTEGNA, SCHOOL OF   Triumph of Divinity

122   MANTEGNA, SCHOOL OF   Triumph of Time   123   MANTEGNA, SCHOOL OF   Triumph of Chastity

124   MANTEGNA, SCHOOL OF   Triumph of Love   125   MANTEGNA, SCHOOL OF   Triumph of Fame

126   MANTEGNA, SCHOOL OF   Triumph of Death

158   MARIOTTO DI NARDO   The Crucifixion

294   MARIOTTO DI NARDO   Madonna and Child
                                    with Saints and Angels

165   MARTINO DI BARTOLOMMEO   The Crucifixion

14   MASACCIO   Profile Portrait of a Young Man

7   MASACCIO   The Madonna of Humility

16   MASOLINO   The Annunciation

336   MASOLINO   The Archangel Gabriel   337   MASOLINO   The Virgin Annunciate

483   MASTER OF THE BAMBINO VISPO   The Adoration of the Magi

329   MASTER OF THE BARBERINI PANELS
              The Annunciation

413   MASTER OF THE JARVES CASSONI
              Madonna and Child with Angels

233   MASTER OF THE JARVES CASSONI   The Journey of the Queen of Sheba

384   MASTER OF THE JARVES CASSONI   The Triumph of Chastity

410   MASTER OF THE LOUVRE PREDELLA   The Annunciation   9   MATTEO DI GIOVANNI   Madonna and Child
                                                                                                     with Angels and Cherubim

389   MATTEO DI GIOVANNI   Judith with the Head of Holofernes   408   MATTEO DI GIOVANNI   Madonna and Child
                                                                                                         with Saints and Angels

310   MAZZOLA-BEDOLI   Portrait of a Monk   362   MEMMI, LIPPO   Madonna and Child

131   MEMMI, LIPPO (?)

II   MEMMI, LIPPO
      Madonna and Child with Donor

Madonna and Child
(Reverse) The Crucifixion

140   MONTAGNA   Madonna and Child   172   MORETTO DA BRESCIA   St. Jerome Peniter

132   MORETTO DA BRESCIA   Madonna and Child with St. Stephen and St. Jerome

341   MORETTO DA BRESCIA   Portrait of a Lady in White

363   MORONE   Madonna and Ecce Homo

143   MORONE   The Adoration of the Magi

547   MORONE   A Dominican Preaching

225   MORONI   A Gentleman in Adoration before the Madonna

309   MORONI   Portrait of a Man   235   NERI DI BICCI   Five Saints

372   NARDO DI CIONE   Madonna and Child with St. Peter
                                 and St. John the Evangelist

431   NERI DI BICCI   The Martyrdom of St. Apollonia

12   NEROCCIO DE' LANDI AND   333   NEROCCIO DE' LANDI   Madonna and Child
       THE MASTER OF THE   with St. Jerome and
       GRISELDA LEGEND   St. Mary Magdalen
       Claudia Quinta

352   NEROCCIO DE' LANDI   The Battle of Actium

504   NICCOLO DA FOLIGNO   The Crucifixion

127   NICCOLÒ DI PIETRO GERINI   The Four Crowned Saints
before Diocletian

432   NICCOLÒ DI PIETRO GERINI
Madonna and Child

6   NUZI AND THE MASTER OF THE FABRIANO ALTARPIECE   Madonna Enthroned
with Saints

201   NUZI   The Resurrection of Drusiana

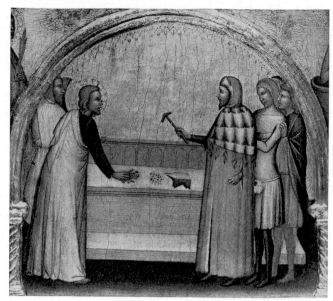

202   NUZI   St. John and the Philosopher Crato

203   NUZI   St. John Converting Atticus and Eugenius

146   ORCAGNA, SCHOOL OF The Coronation of the Virgin

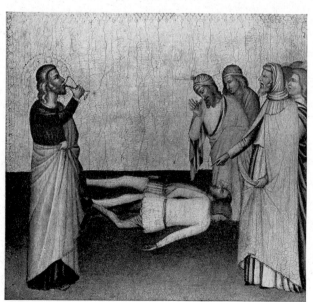

204   NUZI   St. John and the Poisoned Cup

435   PACCHIA   Madonna and Child

442   L'ORTOLANO   The Presentation in the Temple

503   PACCHIAROTTO   Madonna and Child   463   PACCHIAROTTO   Madonna and Child

522   PAOLO FIAMINGO   The Nativity

254   PAOLO VENEZIANO   The Crucifixion

358   PELLEGRINO DI MARIANO   Madonna and Child with Saints

479   PELLEGRINO DI MARIANO   Madonna Enthroned
                                    with Two Saints

27   PERUGINO   The Crucifixion with the Virgin, St. John, St. Jerome, and St. Mary Magdalen

266   PERUGINO   The Annunciation

391   PERUGINO   St. Jerome in the Wilderness

326   PERUGINO   Madonna and Child

428   PERUGINO   St. Bartholomew

220   PESELLINO   The Crucifixion with St. Jerome and St. Francis

317   PIAZZA DA LODI   The Assumption of the Virgin

378   PESELLINO   Madonna and Child

157 PIAZZETTA   A Sleeping Shepherdess

285 PIER FRANCESCO FIORENTINO, PSEUDO-
Madonna and Child

271 PIERO DI COSIMO   Allegory

454 PIERO DI COSIMO   The Visitation with Two Saints

186   PIERO DI COSIMO (?)   Madonna and Child
                                  with Saints and Angels

464   PIERO DI COSIMO   The Nativity with the
                                Infant St. John

114   PIERO DELLA FRANCESCA,
      PROVINCIAL FOLLOWER OF
          Madonna Enthroned with Angels

145   PIETRO DI DOMENICO
      DA MONTEPULCIANO   The Coronation of the Virgin

405   PINTORICCHIO   Portrait of a Youth

141   PINTORICCHIO   Madonna and Child

426   PINTORICCHIO   Madonna Adoring the Child

350 PISAN SCHOOL, XIII CENTURY   Scenes from the
                                       Passion of Christ

23   PISANELLO   Profile Portrait of a Lady

17   POLLAIUOLO, ANTONIO   Portrait of a Man   190   PONTORMO   Portrait of a Young Man

303   PONTORMO   Alessandro de' Medici   480   PONTORMO   The Holy Family

471   PORDENONE   St. Christopher   349   PREDIS   Madonna and Child

180   PUCCINELLI   Tobit Blessing His Son

539   RAFFAELE DEI CARLI   Madonna Enthroned with Saints and Angels

26   RAPHAEL   St. George and the Dragon   25   RAPHAEL   The Niccolini-Cowper Madonna

24   RAPHAEL   The Alba Madonna

534   RAPHAEL   Bindo Altoviti

533   RICCI, SEBASTIANO   The Last Supper

166   RICCI, MARCO and SEBASTIANO   Ruins and Figures

182   RICCI, SEBASTIANO
       A Miracle of St. Francis of Paola

183   RICCI, SEBASTIANO
       The Finding of the True Cross

198   RIMINESE SCHOOL, XIV CENTURY   The Crucifixion

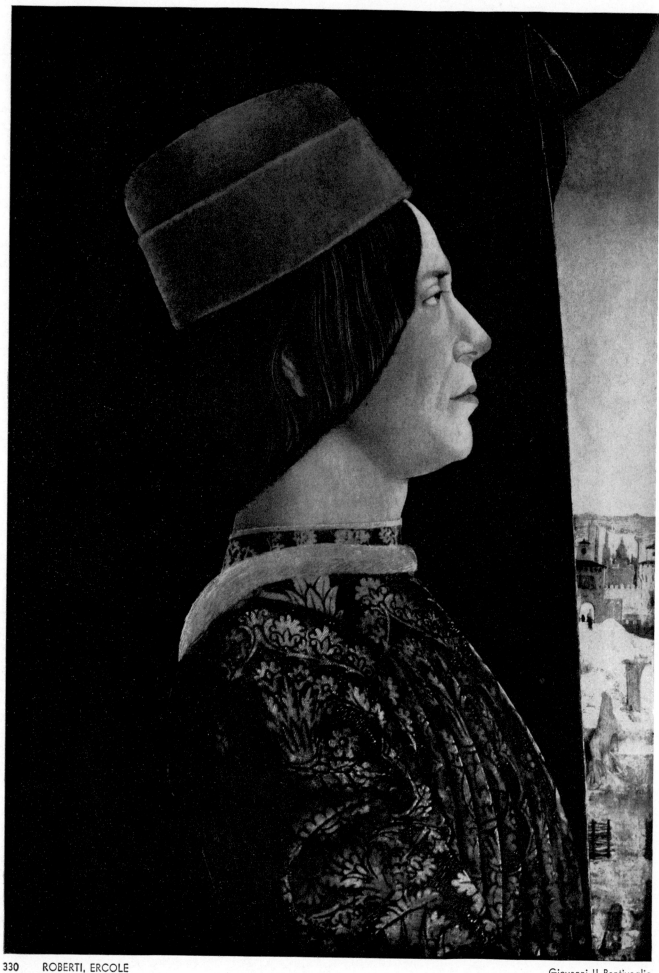

330   ROBERTI, ERCOLE   Giovanni II Bentivoglio

331 ROBERTI, ERCOLE   Ginevra Bentivoglio

465   ROMANINO   Madonna
and Child

451   ROSSELLI, COSIMO   Madonna and Child

430   ROSSELLI, COSIMO   The Adoration of the Child

406   ROSSELLI, COSIMO   The Madonna in Adoration

188   ROSSELLO DI JACOPO FRANCHI   Scene in a Court of Love

218   ROTARI   A Sleeping Girl   219   ROTARI   A Girl with a Flower in Her Hair

189 SALVIATI   Portrait of a Young Woman   296 SALVIATI   Portrait of a Young Man

156 SANO DI PIETRO   The Crucifixion

161   SANO DI PIETRO
St. Augustine

160   SANO DI PIETRO
St. Benedict

274   SANO DI PIETRO   The Adoration of the Child

385   SANO DI PIETRO   Madonna and Child
with Saints and Angels

469   SANTA CROCE, GIROLAMO DA   The Annunciation

357   SASSETTA   Madonna and Child   505   SASSETTA   St. Margaret   506   SASSETTA   St. Apollonia

The Meeting of St. Anthony and St. Paul

322   SCALETTI   Madonna and Child   214   SCHIAVO, PAOLO DI STEFANO   The Flagellation

278   SELLAIO   The Adoration of the Magi

344 SELLAIO Christ Showing the Symbols of the Passion 394 SELLAIO St. John the Baptist

138 SIENESE SCHOOL, XIV CENTURY St. Sigismund of Burgundy 139 SIENESE SCHOOL, XIV CENTURY St. Catherine

259   SIENESE SCHOOL,   Madonna and Child with St. Bartholomew   468   SIENESE SCHOOL,   St. Margaret
       XIV CENTURY   and St. John the Baptist   (NICCOLÒ DI SEGNA ?)

387   SIGNORELLI   The Birth of St. Nicholas of Bari   392   SIGNORELLI   A Miracle of St. Nicholas of Bari

531   SIMONE DEI CROCEFISSI   Madonna and Child with Saints

327   SIMONE MARTINI   The Angel of the Annunciation   402   SIMONE MARTINI   St. John the Baptist

416   SODOMA   Madonna and Child with the Infant St. John

345   SODOMA   Leda and the Swan

444   SODOMA   Three Saints

525   lo SPAGNA   Pietà

236 SPINELLO ARETINO Madonna and Child
with Saints and Angels

163 TADDEO DI BARTOLO St. Geminianus

273 TADDEO DI BARTOLO Madonna and Child

513 TADDEO DI BARTOLO The Coronation of the Virgin

302   TANZIO DA VARALLO   St. Sebastian

117   TIEPOLO, G. B.   The Child Moses Spurns
                                          The Crown of Pharaoh

178   TIEPOLO, G. B.   Portrait of an Actress

179   TIEPOLO, G. B.   A Young Woman with a Parrot

458   TIEPOLO, G. B.   Timocleia and the Thracian Commander

211   TIEPOLO, G. B.   The Apotheosis of a Poet

221   TIEPOLO, G. B.   Portrait of a Youth   243   TINTORETTO   The Trinity Adored by the Heavenly Choir

185   TINTORETTO   Aurora

291   TINTORETTO   The Worship of the Golden Calf

297   TINTORETTO   The Birth of St. John

300   TINTORETTO   Apollo and Marsyas

342   TINTORETTO   Susanna   268   TINTORETTO   Portrait of a Young Man

36   TITIAN   Madonna and Child and the Infant St. John in a Landscape

324   TITIAN   Cupid with the Wheel of Fortune

403 TITIAN   Portrait of a Lady (Giulia di Gonzaga-Colonna?)

34   TITIAN   Venus with a Mirror

370   TITIAN   Allegory (Alfonso d'Este and Laura Diante?)

35   TITIAN   Andrea dei Franceschi

162   TOMMASO DA MODENA   St. Jerome in His Study

450   TURA, COSIMO   Portrait of a Man

409   UCCELLO (?)   Madonna and Child

383   UCCELLO (?)   A Battle Scene

115   UGOLINO DA SIENA   Madonna and Child   215   UGOLINO DA SIENA   Christ Blessing

264   UTILI   A Triumphal Procession

290   UTILI   Portrait of a Boy   456   UTILI   The Adoration of the Child
                                                                                                            with Saints and Donors

434   VANNI, ANDREA   319   VANNI, LIPPO   The Conversion of St. Paul
                St. Clare

222   VANNI, ANDREA   The Adoration of the Magi

257   VECCHIETTA   Pietà

269   VERONESE, PAOLO   The Assumption of the Virgin   38   VERONESE, PAOLO   The Finding of Moses

323   VERONESE, PAOLO   The Baptism of Christ

502 VERROCCHIO Madonna and Child

438   VIVARINI, ALVISE   439   VIVARINI, ALVISE   118   VIVARINI, ANTONIO   St. Catherine Casting
          St. Jerome   St. John the Baptist   Down a Pagan Idol

422   VIVARINI, ALVISE   St. Jerome Reading

229   VIVARINI, BARTOLOMMEO   Madonna and Child   343   VIVARINI, BARTOLOMMEO   The Coronation
                                                                                                                          of the Virgin

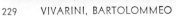

277   ZENALE   Madonna and Saints   382   ZOPPO, MARCO   St. Peter

SPANISH SCHOOLS

85   GOYA   The Marquesa de Pontejos

548   GOYA   Don Bartolomé Sureda

549   GOYA   Doña Teresa Sureda

86   GOYA   Carlos IV of Spain as Huntsman

87   GOYA   Maria Luisa, Queen of Spain

88   GOYA   Señora Sabasa Garcia

84   EL GRECO   St. Martin and the Beggar   81   VELÁZQUEZ   The Needlewoman

80   VELÁZQUEZ   Pope Innocent X   82   VELÁZQUEZ   Portrait of a Young Man

SCULPTURE

French School

A-43   CLODION   Monumental Urn

A-44   CLODION   Monumental Urn

A-42   LEGROS, PIERRE   Cherubs Playing with a Lyre

A-41   TUBI   Cherubs Playing with a Swan

SCULPTURE

Italian Schools

5   AGOSTINO DI DUCCIO   Madonna and Child

A-26   AMADEO   Madonna and Child

9   AMADEO   Lodovico Sforza, called Il Moro

A-10   AMADEO   Gian Galeazzo Sforza

A-25   AMADEO   Kneeling Angel   A-24   AMADEO   Kneeling Angel

A-50   BENEDETTO DA MAIANO   Bust of a
                                        Florentine Statesman

A-62   BERNINI, LORENZO   LOUIS XIV

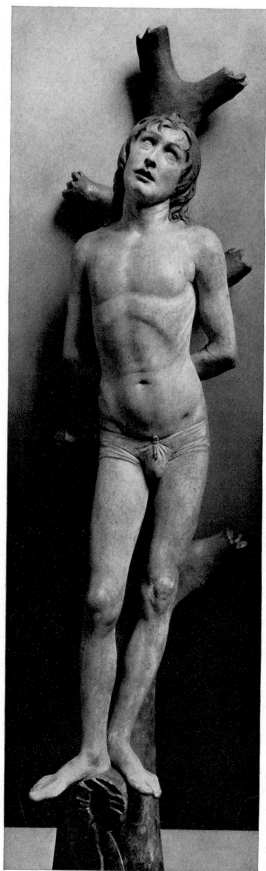

A-3   DESIDERIO DA SETTIGNANO   Madonna and Child

A-51   CIVITALE   St. Sebastian

A-4   DESIDERIO DA   The Young Christ
        SETTIGNANO   with St. John the Baptist

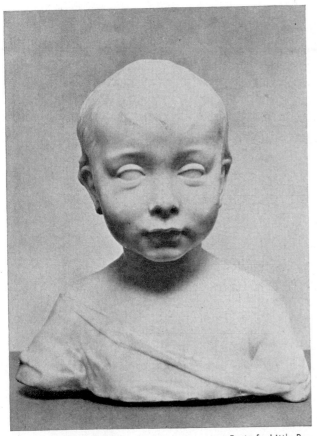

A-2   DESIDERIO DA   Bust of a Little Boy
       SETTIGNANO

A-30   DESIDERIO DA   Bust of a Lady
        SETTIGNANO   (Isotta da Rimini?)

A-18   FLORENTINE SCHOOL,   Bust of a Lady
        XV CENTURY

A-19   DONATELLO   Bust of St. John the Baptist

A-28   FRANCESCO DI SIMONE FERRUCCI   Madonna and Child

A-1   DONATELLO   Madonna and Child   A-23   FONTANA   The Adoration
                                                                                of the Shepherds

A-20   GIOVANNI BOLOGNA   Mercury

A-8   LAURANA   A Princess of
                                the House of Aragon

A-47   LOMBARDO, PIETRO   A Singing Angel   A-32   GAGINI, DOMENICO   The Nativity

A-38   MASTER OF THE   Madonna
       MARBLE MADONNAS   and Child

A-15   MINO DA FIESOLE   Madonna
                             and Child

A-6   MINO DA FIESOLE   Charity

A-7   MINO DA FIESOLE   Faith

A-46   MINO DA FIESOLE   St. Catherine of Siena

A-49   POLLAIUOLO, ANTONIO   Bust of a Warrior

A-40   PYRGOTELES   Madonna and Child with Saints

A-35   della ROBBIA, ANDREA   Bust of the
                                            Christ Child

A-36   della ROBBIA, ANDREA   Bust of St. John
                                            the Baptist

A-13   della ROBBIA, ANDREA   The Virgin
                                            in Adoration

A-12   della ROBBIA, ANDREA   Madonna and Child
        (Atelier)   with God the Father
                                            and Cherubim

A-34   della ROBBIA, LUCA   Madonna and Child

A-48   della ROBBIA, GIOVANNI   Bust of the Young Christ

A-33   della ROBBIA, ANDREA   St. Peter

A-11   della ROBBIA, ANDREA   Madonna and Child
         (Atelier)   with Cherubim

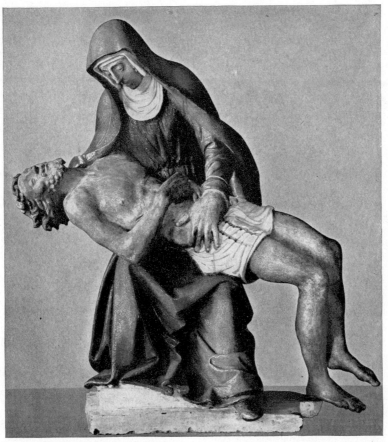

A-45   della ROBBIA, GIOVANNI   Pietà

A-31   ROSSELLINO, ANTONIO   Madonna and Child

A-14   ROSSELLINO, ANTONIO   Madonna and Child

A-22   SANSOVINO, JACOPO   Bacchus and a Young Faun

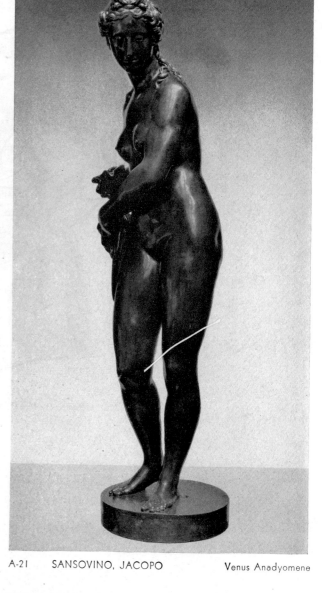

A-21   SANSOVINO, JACOPO   Venus Anadyomene

A-39   TINO DI CAMAINO   Madonna and Child

A-17 VERROCCHIO

Putto Poised on a Globe

A-16   VERROCCHIO   Giuliano de' Medici

A-37   VERROCCHIO   The Adoration of the Shepherds

LIST OF PAINTINGS

Mellon Collection, 1937

NUMBER   PAGE

1. Enthroned Madonna and Child. Byzantine School, XIII Century 78

2. Christ between St. Peter and St. James Major. *Cimabue* (Mentioned 1272-1302). Florentine School 85

3. St. Paul. *Follower of Giotto*, XIV Century. Florentine School 116

4. Madonna Enthroned with Saints and Angels. *Agnolo Gaddi* (Died 1396). Florentine School 106

5. The Madonna of Humility. *Fra Angelico* (1387-1455). Florentine School 57

6. Madonna Enthroned with Saints. *Allegretto Nuzi* (Active 1346-1373/1374) and *Master of the Fabriano Altarpiece* (Work dated 1353). School of Fabriano 159

7. The Madonna of Humility. *Masaccio* (1401-1427/1428). Florentine School 149

8. Nativity with the Prophets Isaiah and Ezekiel. *Duccio di Buoninsegna* (Active 1278-1319). Sienese School 100

9. Madonna and Child with Angels and Cherubim. *Matteo di Giovanni* (c.1430-c.1495). Sienese School 152

10. The Adoration of the Magi. *Benvenuto di Giovanni* (1436-c.1518). Sienese School 72

11. Madonna and Child with Donor. *Lippo Memmi* (Active 1317-1347). Sienese School 153

12. Claudia Quinta. *Neroccio de' Landi* (1447-1500) and *Master of the Griselda Legend* (Active end XV Century). Sienese School 158

13. The Adoration of the Magi. *Giovanni di Paolo* (1403-1482). Sienese School 118

14. Profile Portrait of a Young Man. *Masaccio* (1401-1427/1428). Florentine School 149

15. Matteo Olivieri. *Domenico Veneziano* (c.1400-1461). Florentine School 98

16. The Annunciation. *Masolino da Panicale* (1384-c.1435). Florentine School 149

17. Portrait of a Man. *Antonio Pollaiuolo* (1432-1498). Florentine School 171

18. Madonna Adoring the Child, with an Angel. *Filippino Lippi* (1457-1504). Florentine School 130

19. Portrait of a Youth. *Botticelli* (1444-1510). Florentine School 76

20. Portrait of a Youth. *Filippino Lippi* (1457-1504). Florentine School 130

21. Madonna and Child. *Botticelli* (1444-1510). Florentine School 76

22. The Adoration of the Magi. *Botticelli* (1444-1510). Florentine School 76

23. Profile Portrait of a Lady. *Pisanello* (c.1395-1455). School of Verona 170

24. The Alba Madonna. *Raphael* (1483-1520). Umbrian School 174

25. The Niccolini-Cowper Madonna. *Raphael* (1483-1520). Umbrian School 173

26. St. George and the Dragon. *Raphael* (1483-1520). Umbrian School 173

27. The Crucifixion with the Virgin, St. John, St. Jerome, and St. Mary Magdalen. *Pietro Perugino* (c.1445-1523). Umbrian School 164

28. The Flight into Egypt. *Giovanni Bellini* (c.1430-1516). Venetian School 67

29. Portrait of a Young Man in Red. *Giovanni Bellini* (c.1430-1516). Venetian School 67

30. Madonna and Child. *Antonello da Messina* (1430-1479). Sicilian School 57

31. Portrait of a Young Man. *Antonello da Messina* (1430-1479). Sicilian School 57

32. St. Jerome in the Wilderness. *Andrea Mantegna* (1431-1506). Paduan School 144

33. Madonna and Child with St. Jerome and St. John the Baptist. *Cima da Conegliano* (c.1459-1517/1518). Venetian School 84

34. Venus with a Mirror. *Titian* (c.1477-1576). Venetian School 199

NUMBER		PAGE
35.	Andrea dei Franceschi. *Titian* (c.1477-1576). Venetian School	200
36.	Madonna and Child and the Infant St. John in a Landscape. *Titian* (c.1477-1576). Venetian School	197
37.	Portrait of a Lady. *Bernardino Luini* (c.1480-1532). Milanese School	141
38.	The Finding of Moses. *Paolo Veronese* (1528-1588). Venetian School	204
39.	The Annunciation. *Jan van Eyck* (1380/1400-1441). Flemish School	38
40.	The Nativity. *Petrus Christus* (c.1410-1472/1473). Flemish School	37
41.	Madonna and Child with Angels. *Hans Memling* (c.1430/1435-1494). Flemish School	39
42.	Portrait of a Man with an Arrow. *Hans Memling* (c.1430/1435-1494). Flemish School	39
43.	The Rest on the Flight into Egypt. *Gerard David* (c.1460-1523). Flemish School	37
44.	Portrait of a Lady. *Rogier van der Weyden* (1399/1400-1464). Flemish School	42
45.	Christ Appearing to the Virgin. *Rogier van der Weyden* (1399/1400-1464). Flemish School	42
46.	A Knight of the Order of Calatrava. *Miguel Sithium* (c.1465/1470-1525). Flemish School	40
47.	Isabella Brant. *Peter Paul Rubens* (1577-1640). Flemish School	39
48.	Susanna Fourment and Her Daughter. *Sir Anthony Van Dyck* (1599-1641). Flemish School	40
49.	Marchesa Balbi. *Sir Anthony Van Dyck* (1599-1641). Flemish School	41
50.	Philip, Lord Wharton. *Sir Anthony Van Dyck* (1599-1641). Flemish School	40
51.	William II of Nassau and Orange. *Sir Anthony Van Dyck* (1599-1641). Flemish School	40
52.	Portrait of a Gentleman. *Antonis Mor* (1519-1575). Dutch School	28
53.	The Girl with a Red Hat. *Jan Vermeer* (1632-1675). Dutch School	33
54.	The Lacemaker. *Jan Vermeer* (1632-1675). Dutch School	34
55.	The Smiling Girl. *Jan Vermeer* (1632-1675). Dutch School	34
56.	A Dutch Courtyard. *Pieter de Hooch* (1629-1683). Dutch School	27
57.	The Intruder. *Gabriel Metsu* (c.1629-1667). Dutch School	28
58.	The Suitor's Visit. *Gerard Ter Borch* (1617-1681). Dutch School	32
59.	Herdsmen Tending Cattle. *Aelbert Cuyp* (1620-1691). Dutch School	23
60.	A Farm in the Sunlight. *Meindert Hobbema* (1638-1709). Dutch School	26
61.	A Wooded Landscape. *Meindert Hobbema* (1638-1709). Dutch School	26
62.	A View on a High Road. *Meindert Hobbema* (1638-1709). Dutch School	27
63.	An Old Woman Dozing Over a Book. *Nicolas Maes* (1632-1693). Dutch School	28
64.	Edward VI as Prince of Wales. *Hans Holbein, the Younger* (1497-1543). German School	38
65.	Sir Brian Tuke. *Hans Holbein, the Younger* (1497-1543). German School	38
66.	Portrait of a Man. *Albrecht Dürer* (?) (1471-1528). German School	37
67.	Portrait of an Elderly Lady. *Frans Hals* (c.1580-1666). Dutch School	25
68.	Portrait of an Officer. *Frans Hals* (c.1580-1666). Dutch School	24
69.	Balthasar Coymans. *Frans Hals* (c.1580-1666). Dutch School	24
70.	Portrait of a Man. *Frans Hals* (c.1580-1666). Dutch School	24
71.	Portrait of a Young Man. *Frans Hals* (c.1580-1666). Dutch School	24
72.	Self-Portrait. *Rembrandt Van Ryn* (1606-1669). Dutch School	29
73.	An Old Lady with a Book. *Rembrandt Van Ryn* (1606-1669). Dutch School	30
74.	A Girl with a Broom. *Rembrandt Van Ryn* (1606-1669). Dutch School	30
75.	A Woman Holding a Pink. *Rembrandt Van Ryn* (1606-1669). Dutch School	30
76.	Lucretia. *Rembrandt Van Ryn* (1606-1669). Dutch School	30
77.	A Young Man Seated at a Table. *Rembrandt Van Ryn* (1606-1669). Dutch School	31
78.	A Polish Nobleman. *Rembrandt Van Ryn* (1606-1669). Dutch School	31
79.	Joseph Accused by Potiphar's Wife. *Rembrandt Van Ryn* (1606-1669). Dutch School	31
80.	Pope Innocent X. *Diego de Silva y Velázquez* (1599-1660). Spanish School	216
81.	The Needlewoman. *Diego de Silva y Velázquez* (1599-1660). Spanish School	216
82.	Portrait of a Young Man. *Diego de Silva y Velázquez* (1599-1660). Spanish School	216
83.	St. Ildefonso. *El Greco* (1541-1614). Spanish School	215
84.	St. Martin and the Beggar. *El Greco* (1541-1614). Spanish School	216

NUMBER   PAGE

85. The Marquesa de Pontejos. *Francisco José de Goya y Lucientes* (1746-1828). Spanish School 211

86. Carlos IV of Spain as Huntsman. *Francisco José de Goya y Lucientes* (1746-1828). Spanish School 214

87. Maria Luisa, Queen of Spain. *Francisco José de Goya y Lucientes* (1746-1828). Spanish School 214

88. Señora Sabasa Garcia. *Francisco José de Goya y Lucientes* (1746-1828). Spanish School 214

89. La Camargo Dancing. *Nicolas Lancret* (1690-1743). French School 47

90. The House of Cards. *Jean-Baptiste-Siméon Chardin* (1699-1779). French School 45

91. The Young Governess. *Jean-Baptiste-Siméon Chardin* (1699-1779). French School 46

92. Mrs. Richard Brinsley Sheridan. *Thomas Gainsborough* (1727-1788). British School 15

93. Georgiana, Duchess of Devonshire. *Thomas Gainsborough* (1727-1788). British School 14

94. Lady Broughton. *George Romney* (1734-1802). British School 18

95. Lady Elizabeth Delmé and Her Children. *Sir Joshua Reynolds* (1723-1792). British School 17

96. Lady Templeton and Her Son. *Sir Thomas Lawrence* (1769-1830). British School 16

97. Lady Elizabeth Compton. *Sir Joshua Reynolds* (1723-1792). British School 17

NUMBER   PAGE

98. George IV as Prince of Wales. *Thomas Gainsborough* (1727-1788). British School 14

99. Miss Catherine Tatton. *Thomas Gainsborough* (1727-1788). British School 13

100. Mrs. John Taylor. *Thomas Gainsborough* (1727-1788). British School 13

101. Miss Eleanor Urquhart. *Sir Henry Raeburn* (1756-1823). British School 16

102. Colonel Francis James Scott. *Sir Henry Raeburn* (1756-1823). British School 17

103. John Tait and His Grandson. *Sir Henry Raeburn* (1756-1823). British School 17

104. Miss Willoughby. *George Romney* (1734-1802). British School 18

105. Mrs. Davenport. *George Romney* (1734-1802). British School 18

106. Lady Caroline Howard. *Sir Joshua Reynolds* (1723-1792). British School 18

107. Landscape with a Bridge. *Thomas Gainsborough* (1727-1788). British School 14

108. A View of Salisbury Cathedral. *John Constable* (1776-1837). British School 13

109. Mortlake Terrace. *Joseph Mallord William Turner* (1775-1851). British School 19

110. Approach to Venice. *Joseph Mallord William Turner* (1775-1851). British School 19

111. The Frankland Sisters. *John Hoppner* (1758-1810). British School 16

Kress Collection, 1939

NUMBER   PAGE

112. Crucifix. *Botticelli* (1444-1510). Florentine School 78

113. Taddeo Taddei. *Ridolfo Ghirlandaio* (1483-1561). Florentine School 111

114. Madonna Enthroned with Angels. *Provincial Follower of Piero della Francesca* (Active c.1450). Central Italian School 168

115. Madonna and Child. *Ugolino da Siena* (Active 1317-1327). Sienese School 201

116. Madonna and Child with Angels. *Giovanni di Niccolò da Pisa* (Mentioned 1358 and 1360). Pisan-Sienese School 117

117. The Child Moses Spurns the Crown of Pharaoh. *Giovanni Battista Tiepolo* (1696-1770). Venetian School 192

118. St. Catherine Casting Down a Pagan Idol. *Antonio Vivarini* (Active 1441-1476/1484). Venetian School 206

NUMBER   PAGE

119. St. John the Evangelist. *Pseudo-Boccaccino* (Beginning of XVI Century). Lombard School 73

120. St. Matthew. *Pseudo-Boccaccino* (Beginning of XVI Century). Lombard School 73

121. Triumph of Divinity. *School of Mantegna* (c.1500). Paduan School 146

122. Triumph of Time. *School of Mantegna* (c.1500). Paduan School 146

123. Triumph of Chastity. *School of Mantegna* (c.1500). Paduan School 146

124. Triumph of Love. *School of Mantegna* (c.1500). Paduan School 147

125. Triumph of Fame. *School of Mantegna* (c.1500). Paduan School 147

126. Triumph of Death. *School of Mantegna* (c.1500). Paduan School 147

NUMBER | PAGE

127. The Four Crowned Saints before Diocletian. *Niccolò di Pietro Gerini* (Active 1368-1414). Florentine School _____ 159

128. St. John Preaching. *Benedetto Bembo* (Mentioned 1462-1475). Lombard School _____ 72

129. Prudence. *Vittore Carpaccio* (c.1455-1523/ 1526). Venetian School _____ 80

130. Madonna and Child with Saints and Donor. Lombard School, XV Century _____ 133

131. Madonna and Child. (Reverse) The Crucifixion. *Lippo Memmi* (?) (Active 1317-1347). Sienese School _____ 153

132. Madonna and Child with St. Stephen and St. Jerome. *Moretto da Brescia* (c.1498-1554). Brescian School _____ 154

133. Temperance. *Vittore Carpaccio* (c.1455-1523/ 1526). Venetian School _____ 80

134. The Crucifixion. *Follower of Pietro Lorenzetti* (Middle XIV Century). Sienese School _____ 135

135. The Interior of the Pantheon. *Giovanni Paolo Panini* (1691/1692-1765). Roman School _____ 162

136. The Crucifixion. *Luca di Tommè* (Active 1355-1389). Sienese School _____ 139

137. Christ on the Road to Calvary. *Paolo di Giovanni Fei* (Mentioned 1372-1410). Sienese School _____ 101

138. St. Sigismund of Burgundy. Sienese School, XIV Century _____ 187

139. St. Catherine. Sienese School, XIV Century _____ 187

140. Madonna and Child. *Bartolommeo Montagna* (c.1450-1523). School of Vicenza _____ 154

141. Madonna and Child. *Pintoricchio* (c.1454-1513). Umbrian School _____ 170

142. Portrait of a Young Woman. *Giuliano Bugiardini* (1475-1554). Florentine School _____ 78

143. The Adoration of the Magi. *Domenico Morone* (c.1442-after 1517). School of Verona _____ 155

144. Madonna and Child with the Infant St. John. *Antonello da Saliba* (c.1466-1535). Sicilian School _____ 58

145. The Coronation of the Virgin. *Pietro di Domenico da Montepulciano* (Active after 1415). School of the Marches _____ 168

146. The Coronation of the Virgin. *School of Orcagna*, XIV Century. Florentine School _____ 160

147. St. Francis. *Carlo Crivelli* (1430/1435-after 1493). Venetian School _____ 92

148. St. Nicodemus (?). *Carlo Crivelli* (1430/1435-after 1493). Venetian School _____ 92

149. Madonna and Child with Saints. *Jacopo di Cione* (Mentioned 1368-1398). Florentine School _____ 126

NUMBER | PAGE

150. A Tribute to Apollo. *Bartolommeo di Giovanni* (Mentioned 1488). Florentine School _____ 63

151. A King with His Counsellors. *Bartolommeo di Giovanni* (Mentioned 1488). Florentine School _____ 63

152. The Presentation in the Temple. *Andrea di Bartolo* (Active 1389-1428). Sienese School _____ 53

153. The Nativity of the Virgin. *Andrea di Bartolo* (Active 1389-1428). Sienese School _____ 53

154. Joachim and the Beggars. *Andrea di Bartolo* (Active 1389-1428). Sienese School _____ 53

155. Portrait of a Woman. *Vincenzo Catena* (c.1470-1531). Venetian School _____ 83

156. The Crucifixion. *Sano di Pietro* (1406-1481). Sienese School _____ 182

157. A Sleeping Shepherdess. *Giovanni Battista Piazzetta* (1682-1754). Venetian School _____ 167

158. The Crucifixion. *Mariotto di Nardo* (Mentioned 1394-1424). Florentine School _____ 148

159. Portrait of a Youth. *Alessandro Allori* (1535-1607). Florentine School _____ 52

160. St. Benedict. *Sano di Pietro* (1406-1481). Sienese School _____ 183

161. St. Augustine. *Sano di Pietro* (1406-1481). Sienese School _____ 183

162. St. Jerome in His Study. *Tommaso da Modena* (1325/1326-1379). School of Modena _____ 200

163. St. Geminianus. *Taddeo di Bartolo* (c.1362-1422). Sienese School _____ 191

164. St. Mary Magdalen. *Ugolino Lorenzetti* (Active 1320-1335). Sienese School _____ 136

165. The Crucifixion. *Martino di Bartolommeo* (Mentioned 1389-1434). Sienese School _____ 148

166. Ruins and Figures. *Sebastiano Ricci* (1659-1734) and *Marco Ricci* (1676-1729). Venetian School _____ 176

167. St. Augustine and the Three Catechumens. *Girolamo Genga* (c.1476-1551). Umbrian School _____ 109

168. Madonna and Child. *Gualtieri di Giovanni* (Mentioned 1389-1445). Sienese School _____ 123

169. A Scene from the Life of St. Nicholas. Florentine School, XVI Century _____ 102

170. Portrait of a Boy in Red. *Alessandro Allori* (1535-1607). Florentine School _____ 51

171. Diana. *Paris Bordone* (1500-1571). Venetian School _____ 75

172. St. Jerome Penitent. *Moretto da Brescia* (c.1498-1554). Brescian School _____ 154

173. Cupids with Sleeping Nymphs. *Giuseppe Maria Crespi* (1665-1747). School of Bologna _____ 91

NUMBER		PAGE

174. The Simulated Faint. *Pietro Longhi* (1702-1785). Venetian School — 133

175. Blind Man's Buff. *Pietro Longhi* (1702-1785). Venetian School — 134

176. Madonna and Child with Saints and Angels. *Mariotto Albertinelli* (1474-1515) and *Fra Bartolommeo* (1472-1517). Florentine School — 51

177. Sir John Reade, Bart. *Rosalba Carriera* (1675-1757). Venetian School — 83

178. Portrait of an Actress. *Giovanni Battista Tiepolo* (1696-1770). Venetian School — 192

179. A Young Woman with a Parrot. *Giovanni Battista Tiepolo* (1696-1770). Venetian School — 192

180. Tobit Blessing His Son. *Angelo Puccinelli* (Active 1350-1399). Sienese School — 172

181. The Annunciation with Donor. *Agnolo Gaddi* (Died 1396). Florentine School — 107

182. A Miracle of St. Francis of Paola. *Sebastiano Ricci* (1659-1734). Venetian School — 177

183. The Finding of the True Cross. *Sebastiano Ricci* (1659-1734). Venetian School — 177

184. Madonna and Child. *Francesco Francia* (c.1450-1517). Ferrarese-Bolognese School — 105

185. Aurora. *Jacopo Tintoretto* (1518-1594). Venetian School — 195

186. Madonna and Child with Saints and Angels. *Piero di Cosimo* (?) (1462-c.1521). Florentine School — 168

187. Madonna and Child with Angels. *Guidoccio Cozzarelli* (Mentioned 1450-1499). Sienese School — 91

188. Scene in a Court of Love. *Rossello di Jacopo Franchi* (c.1376-1457). Florentine School — 181

189. Portrait of a Young Woman. *Francesco Salviati* (1510-1563). Florentine School — 182

190. Portrait of a Young Man. *Pontormo* (1494-c.1556). Florentine School — 171

191. St. Peter. *Michele Giambono* (Mentioned 1420-1462). Venetian School — 112

192. St. Paul and St. Augustine. *Giusto de' Menabuoi* (Active 1363-1393). Florentine School — 121

193. Madonna and Child between Two Angels, St. Francis and St. Louis. *Paolo di Giovanni Fei* (Mentioned 1372-1410). Sienese School — 101

194. The Mystic Marriage of St. Catherine. *Correggio* (1489/1494-1534). School of Parma — 87

195. The Flagellation. *Bernardo Daddi* (Mentioned 1312/1320-c.1348). Florentine School — 94

196. St. Catherine. *Bernardo Daddi* (Mentioned 1312/1320-c.1348). Florentine School — 94

197. St. Anthony Abbot. *Giovanni da Milano* (Active 1350-1369). Milanese-Florentine School — 117

NUMBER		PAGE

198. The Crucifixion. School of Rimini, First half XIV Century — 177

199. The Parable of Dives and Lazarus. *Domenico Feti* (c.1589-1624). Roman School — 102

200. Madonna and Child with Saints. *Follower of Bernardo Daddi* (c.1350). Florentine School — 95

201. The Resurrection of Drusiana. *Allegretto Nuzi* (Active 1346-1373/1374). School of Fabriano — 160

202. St. John and the Philosopher Crato. *Allegretto Nuzi* (Active 1346-1373/1374). School of Fabriano — 160

203. St. John Converting Atticus and Eugenius. *Allegretto Nuzi* (Active 1346-1373/1374). School of Fabriano — 160

204. St. John and the Poisoned Cup. *Allegretto Nuzi*. (Active 1346-1373/1374). School of Fabriano — 160

205. Portrait of a Musician. *Bernardino Licinio* (c.1489-before 1565). Venetian School — 128

206. The Crowning of St. Catherine of Alexandria. *Bonifazio Veronese* (c.1487-1553). Venetian School — 75

207. Portrait of a Man. *Lorenzo Lotto* (c.1480-1556). Venetian School — 137

208. St. Francis in Glory. *Filippino Lippi* and *Assistants* (Second half XV Century). Florentine School — 128

209. The Standard Bearer. *Dosso Dossi* (c.1479-c.1542). Ferrarese School — 99

210. Portrait of a Young Man. *Franciabigio* (c.1482-1525). Florentine School — 105

211. The Apotheosis of a Poet. *Giovanni Battista Tiepolo* (1696-1770). Venetian School — 194

212. The Baptism of Christ. *Garofalo* (1481-1559). Ferrarese School — 108

213. Portrait of a Young Man. *Vittore Ghislandi* (1655-1743). School of Bergamo — 111

214. The Flagellation. *Paolo di Stefano Schiavo* (1397-1478). Florentine School — 186

215. Christ Blessing. *Ugolino da Siena* (Active 1317-1327). Sienese School — 201

216. The Adoration of the Child. *Gaudenzio Ferrari* (c.1480-1546). Lombard School — 108

217. Venus and Cupid. *Matteo Balducci* (Mentioned 1509-c.1555). Umbrian-Sienese School — 61

218. A Sleeping Girl. *Pietro Rotari* (1707-1762). Venetian School — 181

219. A Girl with a Flower in Her Hair. *Pietro Rotari* (1707-1762). Venetian School — 181

220. The Crucifixion with St. Jerome and St. Francis. *Francesco Pesellino* (1422-1457). Florentine School — 166

NUMBER | PAGE

221. Portrait of a Youth. *Giovanni Battista Tiepolo* (1696-1770). Venetian School _____ 194

222. The Adoration of the Magi. *Andrea Vanni* (c.1332-c.1414). Sienese School _____ 203

223. The Assumption of the Virgin. *Andrea di Giusto* (Active 1424-1455). Florentine School 54

224. View on the Cannareggio, Venice. *Francesco Guardi* (1712-1793). Venetian School ____ 124

225. A Gentleman in Adoration before the Madonna. *Giovanni Battista Moroni* (c.1520 - 1578). Brescian School _____ 156

226. Madonna and Child with Angels. *Francesco del Cossa* (c.1435-1477). Ferrarese School ____ 88

227. Madonna and Child with Two Saints. *Vittore Carpaccio* (c.1455 - 1523/1526). Venetian School _____ 81

228. St. Catherine. *Lorenzo Lotto* (c.1480-1556). Venetian School _____ 137

229. Madonna and Child. *Bartolommeo Vivarini* (Active 1450-1499). Venetian School _____ 207

230. The Martyrdom of St. Lucy. *Bernardino Fungai* (c.1460-1516). Umbrian-Sienese School ____ 106

231. Venus. *Bernardino Luini* (c.1480-1532). Milanese School _____ 139

232. Madonna and Child with Angels. Florentine School, XV Century _____ 102

233. The Journey of the Queen of Sheba. *Master of the Jarves Cassoni* (Active c.1450). Florentine School _____ 151

234. A View of the Ducal Palace, Venice. *Canaletto* (1697-1768). Venetian School _____ 79

235. Five Saints. *Neri di Bicci* (1419-c.1491). Florentine School _____ 157

236. Madonna and Child with Saints and Angels. *Spinello Aretino* (c.1346-1410). Florentine School _____ 191

237. The Annunciation to the Shepherds. *Jacopo Bassano* (1510/1515-1592). Venetian School 65

238. Madonna and Child, St. John the Baptist, and St. Catherine. *Giovanni del Biondo* (Active 1356-1392). Florentine School _____ 117

239. Madonna and Child with Saints and Angels. *Agnolo Gaddi* (Died 1396). Florentine School 107

240. Campo San Zanipolo. *Francesco Guardi* (1712-1793). Venetian School _____ 125

241. The Crucifixion. *Andrea da Firenze* (Active 1343-1377). Florentine School _____ 53

242. The Baptism of Christ. *Giovanni Baronzio* (Works dated 1344 and 1345). School of Rimini _____ 62

NUMBER | PAGE

243. The Trinity Adored by the Heavenly Choir. *Jacopo Tintoretto* (1518-1594). Venetian School _____ 194

244. Madonna and Child with St. John and Angels. *Sebastiano Mainardi* (c.1450-1513). Florentine School _____ 144

245. Madonna and Child. *Cenni di Francesco* (Mentioned 1410 and 1415). Florentine School ____ 84

246. A Judgment Scene. *Andrea di Giusto* (Active 1424-1455). Florentine School _____ 54

247. Allegory of Painting. *Rosalba Carriera* (1675-1757). Venetian School _____ 83

248. Scenes from a Legend. Florentine School, XV Century _____ 102

249. Madonna and Child with St. Jerome. *Benedetto Diana* (Mentioned 1482-1525). Venetian School _____ 97

250. Madonna and Child with Saints. *Pietro Lorenzetti* (Active c.1305-c.1348). Sienese School ____ 134

251. St. Francis Receiving the Stigmata. *Domenico Veneziano* (c.1400-1461). Florentine School 98

252. The Calling of the Apostles Peter and Andrew. *Duccio di Buoninsegna* (Active 1278-1319). Sienese School _____ 100

253. Venus and Cupid in a Landscape. *Giorgione* (?) (1478-1510). Venetian School _____ 114

254. The Crucifixion. *Paolo Veneziano* (Mentioned 1333-1362). Venetian School _____ 163

255. Madonna Adoring the Child. *Marco Basaiti* (Active 1503-1530). Venetian School _____ 64

256. The Meeting of St. Francis and St. Dominic. *Fra Angelico* (1387-1455). Florentine School 57

257. Pietà. *Lorenzo Vecchietta* (c.1412-1480). Sienese School _____ 203

258. A Maiden's Dream. *Lorenzo Lotto* (c.1480-1556). Venetian School _____ 138

259. Madonna and Child with St. Bartholomew and St. John the Baptist. Sienese School, XIV Century _____ 188

260. St. Nicholas (?). *Vittore Carpaccio* (c.1455-1523/1526). Venetian School _____ 81

261. St. Peter Martyr. *Vittore Carpaccio* (c.1455-1523/1526). Venetian School _____ 81

262. The Dead Christ with Madonna, St. John, and Donor. *Jacopo di Cione* (Mentioned 1368-1398). Florentine School _____ 127

263. The Madonna of the Carnation. *Bernardino Luini* (c.1480-1532). Milanese School _____ 141

264. A Triumphal Procession. *Giovanni Battista Utili* (Mentioned 1498-1515). Florentine School ____ 201

265. Madonna and Child with Saints. *Giovanni dal Ponte* (1385-1437). Florentine School _____ 120

NUMBER   PAGE

266. The Annunciation. *Pietro Perugino* (c.1445-
     1523). Umbrian School_____ 164

267. Allegory. *Lorenzo Lotto* (c.1480-1556). Ve-
     netian School _____ 138

268. Portrait of a Young Man. *Jacopo Tintoretto*
     (1518-1594). Venetian School_____ 196

269. The Assumption of the Virgin. *Paolo Veronese*
     (1528-1588). Venetian School_____ 204

270. Still Life. *Michelangelo Caravaggio* (1573-
     1610). Roman School_____ 79

271. Allegory. *Piero di Cosimo* (1462-c.1521).
     Florentine School _____ 167

272. Allegory. *Bacchiacca* (1494-1557). Florentine
     School _____ 60

273. Madonna and Child. *Taddeo di Bartolo*
     (c.1362-1422). Sienese School_____ 191

274. The Adoration of the Child. *Sano di Pietro*
     (1406-1481). Sienese School_____ 183

275. The Prodigal Son (?). *Giuseppe Bazzani*
     (c.1690-1769). School of Mantua_____ 65

276. Quintilia Fischieri. *Federico Barocci* (or *Bar-
     occio*) (1535-1612). Roman School_____ 62

277. Madonna and Saints. *Bernardino Zenale* (1436-
     1526). Lombard School_____ 207

278. The Adoration of the Magi. *Jacopo del Sellaio*
     (1441/1442-1493). Florentine School_____ 186

279. St. Jerome in the Wilderness. *Cima da Coneg-
     liano* (c.1459-1517/1518). Venetian School_____ 85

280. The Crucifixion with St. Francis. *Antoniazzo
     Romano* (Active 1461-1508/1512). Roman
     School _____ 58

281. St. Nicholas of Tolentino and St. Christopher.
     Lorenzo Costa (c.1460-1535). Ferrarese-
     Bolognese School _____ 89

282. St. Julianus and St. Vincent. *Lorenzo Costa*
     (c.1460-1535). Ferrarese-Bolognese School____ 89

283. St. Catherine and St. Roch. *Lorenzo Costa*
     (c.1460-1535). Ferrarese-Bolognese School____ 89

284. St. Sebastian and St. Lucy. *Lorenzo Costa*
     (c.1460-1535). Ferrarese-Bolognese School____ 89

285. Madonna and Child. *Pseudo-Pier Francesco
     Fiorentino* (Late XV Century). Florentine
     School _____ 167

286. Madonna and Child in a Landscape. *Lattanzio
     da Rimini* (Mentioned 1492). Venetian School 127

287. Madonna and Child. *Marco Basaiti* (Active
     1503-1530). Venetian School_____ 65

288. The Capture of Christ in the Garden. *Cimabue*
     (?) (Mentioned 1272-1302). Florentine School 85

289. Judith with the Head of Holofernes. *Andrea
     Mantegna* (1431-1506). Paduan School _____ 144

NUMBER   PAGE

290. Portrait of a Boy. *Giovanni Battista Utili* (Men-
     tioned 1498-1515). Florentine School_____ 202

291. The Worship of the Golden Calf. *Jacopo Tin-
     toretto* (1518-1594). Venetian School_____ 195

292. The Holy Family with St. Catherine. *Francesco
     Guardi* (1712-1793). Venetian School_____ 124

293. Portrait of a Young Man. *Giovanni Bellini*
     (c.1430-1516). Venetian School_____ 67

294. Madonna and Child with Saints and Angels.
     Mariotto di Nardo. (Mentioned 1394-1424).
     Florentine School _____ 148

295. Madonna and Child. *Bramantino* (Active
     1503-1536). Milanese School_____ 78

296. Portrait of a Young Man. *Francesco Salviati*
     (1510-1563). Florentine School_____ 182

297. The Birth of St. John. *Jacopo Tintoretto*
     (1518-1594). Venetian School_____ 196

298. St. Donatus. *Filippino Lippi* (1457-1504). Flor-
     entine School _____ 128

299. St. Augustine. *Filippino Lippi* (1457-1504).
     Florentine School _____ 128

300. Apollo and Marsyas. *Jacopo Tintoretto* (1518-
     1594). Venetian School_____ 196

301. A Laughing Man. *Giuseppe Bazzani* (c.1690-
     1769). School of Mantua_____ 66

302. St. Sebastian. *Tanzio da Varallo* (c.1574-
     c.1635). North Italian School_____ 192

303. Alessandro de' Medici. *Pontormo* (1494-
     c.1556). Florentine School_____ 171

304. St. Stephen. *Vittore Carpaccio* (c.1455-1523/
     1526). Venetian School_____ 81

305. St. John the Baptist. *Vittore Carpaccio* (c.1455-
     1523/1526). Venetian School_____ 81

306. Madonna and Child with the Infant St. John.
     Francesco Francia (c.1450-1517). Ferrarese-
     Bolognese School _____ 104

307. Portrait of a Man. *Vincenzo Catena* (c.1470-
     1531). Venetian School_____ 83

308. Portrait of a Monk. *Giovanni Boccati* (Men-
     tioned 1445-1480). Umbrian School_____ 73

309. Portrait of a Man. *Giovanni Battista Moroni*
     (c.1520-1578). Brescian School_____ 157

310. Portrait of a Monk. *Girolamo Mazzola-Bedoli*
     (c.1500-1569). School of Parma_____ 153

311. The Last Supper. *Cimabue* (?) (Mentioned
     1272-1302). Florentine School_____ 86

312. Pietà. *Antonio da Viterbo* (Active 1478-1509).
     Umbrian School _____ 59

313. The Adoration of the Magi. *Bartolommeo di
     Giovanni* (Mentioned 1488). Florentine School 64

NUMBER   PAGE

314. The Coronation of the Virgin. *Agnolo Gaddi*
      (Died 1396). Florentine School _____ 107

315. Abraham Visited by the Angels. *Antonello da
      Saliba* (c.1466-1535). Sicilian School _____ 58

316. Portrait of a Man. *Giovanni Bellini* (c.1430-
      1516). Venetian School _____ 68

317. The Assumption of the Virgin. *Albertino Piazza
      da Lodi* (c.1475-1529). Lombard School _____ 166

318. Processional Cross. *Alunno di Benozzo* (XV
      Century). Florentine School _____ 51

319. The Conversion of St. Paul. *Lippo Vanni*
      (Active 1341-1375). Sienese School _____ 202

320. St. Francis. *Vittore Crivelli* (Active 1481-
      c.1501). Venetian School _____ 92

321. St. Louis of France. *Bernardino Fungai* (c.1460-
      1516). Umbrian-Sienese School _____ 105

322. Madonna and Child. *Leonardo Scaletti* (Ac-
      tive 1458-1495). Ferrarese School _____ 186

323. The Baptism of Christ. *Paolo Veronese* (1528-
      1588). Venetian School _____ 204

324. Cupid with the Wheel of Fortune. *Titian*
      (c.1477-1576). Venetian School _____ 197

325. Madonna and Child. *Alesso Baldovinetti* (1425-
      1499). Florentine School _____ 60

326. Madonna and Child. *Pietro Perugino* (c.1445-
      1523). Umbrian School _____ 165

327. The Angel of the Annunciation. *Simone Martini*
      (c.1284-1344). Sienese School _____ 189

328. St. Jerome Reading. *Giovanni Bellini* (c.1430-
      1516). Venetian School _____ 68

329. The Annunciation. *Master of the Barberini
      Panels* (Active Middle XV Century). Floren-
      tine School (?) _____ 151

330. Giovanni II Bentivoglio. *Ercole Roberti*
      (c.1456-1496). Ferrarese School _____ 178

331. Ginevra Bentivoglio. *Ercole Roberti* (c.1456-
      1496). Ferrarese School _____ 179

332. Madonna and Child. *Domenico Veneziano*
      (c.1400-1461). Florentine School _____ 98

333. Madonna and Child with St. Jerome and St.
      Mary Magdalen. *Neroccio de' Landi* (1447-
      1500). Sienese School _____ 158

334. The Annunciation. *Giovanni di Paolo* (1403-
      1482). Sienese School _____ 118

335. Portrait of a Condottiere. *Giovanni Bellini*
      (c.1430-1516). Venetian School _____ 69

336. The Archangel Gabriel. *Masolino da Panicale*
      (1384-c.1435). Florentine School _____ 150

337. The Virgin Annunciate. *Masolino da Panicale*
      (1384-c.1435). Florentine School _____ 150

NUMBER   PAGE

338. St. Liberal. *Francesco del Cossa* (c.1435-1477).
      Ferrarese School _____ 88

339. St. Lucy. *Francesco del Cossa* (c.1435-1477).
      Ferrarese School _____ 88

340. Tobias and the Angel. *Filippino Lippi* (1457-
      1504). Florentine School _____ 129

341. Portrait of a Lady in White. *Moretto da Brescia*
      (c.1498-1554). Brescian School _____ 155

342. Susanna. *Jacopo Tintoretto* (1518-1594).
      Venetian School _____ 196

343. The Coronation of the Virgin. *Bartolommeo
      Vivarini* (Active 1450-1499). Venetian School 207

344. Christ Showing the Symbols of the Passion.
      Jacopo del Sellaio (1441/1442-1493). Flor-
      entine School _____ 187

345. Leda and the Swan. *Sodoma* (1477-1549).
      Sienese School _____ 190

346. Portrait of a Young Girl. *Correggio* (1489/
      1494-1534). School of Parma _____ 87

347. The Coronation of the Virgin. *Giovanni da
      Bologna* (Mentioned 1377-1389). School of
      Bologna _____ 117

348. St. Paul. *Antonio Veneziano* (Active 1370-
      1387). Florentine School _____ 59

349. Madonna and Child. *Ambrogio de' Predis*
      (Mentioned 1472-1508). Milanese School _____ 172

350. Scenes from the Passion of Christ. Pisan
      School, XIII Century _____ 170

351. Madonna and Child with Saints and Angels.
      Giovanni di Paolo (1403-1482). Sienese School 118

352. The Battle of Actium. *Neroccio de' Landi*
      (1447-1500). Sienese School _____ 158

353. The Visit of Cleopatra to Antony. *Francesco di
      Giorgio* (1439-1502). Sienese School _____ 103

354. Two Saints. *Fra Diamante* (1430-c.1498).
      Florentine School _____ 96

355. Two Saints. *Fra Diamante* (1430-c.1498).
      Florentine School _____ 96

356. Madonna and Child. *Correggio* (?) (1489/
      1494-1534). School of Parma _____ 88

357. Madonna and Child. *Sassetta* (Active 1423-
      1450). Sienese School _____ 184

358. Madonna and Child with Saints. *Pellegrino di
      Mariano* (Active 1449-1492). Sienese School _ 163

359. The Presentation in the Temple. *Jacopo del
      Casentino* (Active 1339-1349/1358). Floren-
      tine School _____ 126

360. St. Clare. *Pietro Lorenzetti* (Active c.1305-
      c.1348). Sienese School _____ 134

361. Scene from a Legend. *Dosso Dossi* (c.1479-
      c.1542). Ferrarese School _____ 99

NUMBER		PAGE

362. Madonna and Child. *Lippo Memmi* (Active 1317-1347). Sienese School _____ 153

363. Madonna and Ecce Homo. *Domenico Morone* (c.1442-after 1517). School of Verona _____ 155

364. St. Paul. *Lorenzo Costa* (c.1460-1535). Ferrarese-Bolognese School _____ 90

365. Portrait of a Venetian Gentleman. *Giovanni Bellini* (c.1430-1516). Venetian School _____ 70

366. Madonna and Child. *Gentile da Fabriano* (c.1360-1427). Umbrian School _____ 110

367. Madonna and Child. *Giotto* (c. 1266-1336). Florentine School _____ 115

368. Portrait of a Gentleman. *Bartolommeo Veneto* (Active 1502-1530). Lombard-Venetian School 64

369. Portrait of a Venetian Gentleman. *Giorgione* (1478-1510) and *Titian* (c.1477-1576). Venetian School _____ 114

370. Allegory (Alfonso d'Este and Laura Diante?). *Titian* (c.1477-1576). Venetian School _____ 199

371. The Entombment. *Fra Angelico* (1387-1455). Florentine School _____ 56

372. Madonna and Child with St. Peter and St. John the Evangelist. *Nardo di Cione* (Active 1345-1366). Florentine School _____ 157

373. Madonna and Child in a Landscape. *Giovanni Bellini* (c.1430-1516). Venetian School _____ 70

374. Profile Portrait of a Boy. *Jacopo Bellini* (c.1400-1470/1471). Venetian School _____ 71

375. Madonna and Child. *Carlo Crivelli* (1430/1435-after 1493). Venetian School _____ 93

376. St. Ursula with Angels and Donor. *Benozzo Gozzoli* (1420-1497). Florentine School _____ 122

377. Madonna and Child. *Andrea Mantegna* (1431-1506). Paduan School _____ 145

378. Madonna and Child. *Francesco Pesellino* (1422-1457). Florentine School _____ 166

379. A Miracle of St. Nicholas. *Gentile da Fabriano* (c.1360-1427). Umbrian School _____ 109

380. St. Dominic. *Domenico Ghirlandaio* (1449-1494). Florentine School _____ 111

381. St. Michael. *Domenico Ghirlandaio* (1449-1494). Florentine School _____ 111

382. St. Peter. *Marco Zoppo* (1433-c.1478). Ferrarese School _____ 207

383. A Battle Scene. *Paolo Uccello* (?) (c.1397-1475). Florentine School _____ 201

384. The Triumph of Chastity. *Master of the Jarves Cassoni* (Active c.1450). Florentine School _____ 151

385. Madonna and Child with Saints and Angels. *Sano di Pietro* (1406-1481). Sienese School _____ 183

386. St. Christopher. *Vincenzo Foppa* (1427/1430-1515/1516). Lombard School _____ 103

387. The Birth of St. Nicholas of Bari. *Luca Signorelli* (c.1441-1523). Umbrian School _____ 188

388. Madonna and Child. *Barnaba da Modena* (Active 1361-1383). Modenese School _____ 61

389. Judith with the Head of Holofernes. *Matteo di Giovanni* (c.1430-1495). Sienese School _____ 152

390. The Nativity. *Fra Filippo Lippi* (c.1406-1469). Florentine School _____ 132

391. St. Jerome in the Wilderness. *Pietro Perugino* (c.1445-1523). Umbrian School _____ 164

392. A Miracle of St. Nicholas of Bari. *Luca Signorelli* (c.1441-1523). Umbrian School _____ 188

393. The Assumption of the Virgin. *Giovanni di Paolo* (1403-1482). Sienese School _____ 119

394. St. John the Baptist. *Jacopo del Sellaio* (1441/1442-1493). Florentine School _____ 187

395. The Miracle of the Catafalque. *Lorenzo Costa* (c.1460-1535). Ferrarese-Bolognese School _____ 90

396. The Miracle of the Catafalque. *Lorenzo Costa* (c.1460-1535). Ferrarese-Bolognese School _____ 90

397. The Miracle of the Catafalque. *Lorenzo Costa* (c.1460-1535). Ferrarese-Bolognese School _____ 90

398. Two Saints. *Fra Diamante* (1430-c.1498). Florentine School _____ 96

399. The Nativity. *Lorenzo Lotto* (c.1480-1556). Venetian School _____ 138

400. The Adoration of the Shepherds. *Giorgione* (1478-1510). Venetian School _____ 113

401. Madonna and Child. *Fra Filippo Lippi* (c.1406-1469). Florentine School _____ 131

402. St. John the Baptist. *Simone Martini* (c.1284-1344). Sienese School _____ 189

403. Portrait of a Lady (Giulia di Gonzaga-Colonna?). *Titian* (c.1477-1576). Venetian School 198

404. The Meeting of St. Anthony and St. Paul. *Sassetta* (Active 1423-1450). Sienese School _____ 185

405. Portrait of a Youth. *Pintoricchio* (c.1454-1513). Umbrian School _____ 169

406. The Madonna in Adoration. *Cosimo Rosselli* (1439-1507). Florentine School _____ 180

407. Head of the Madonna. *Fra Filippo Lippi* (c.1406-1469). Florentine School _____ 133

408. Madonna and Child with Saints and Angels. *Matteo di Giovanni* (c.1430-1495). Sienese School _____ 152

409. Madonna and Child. *Paolo Uccello* (?) (c.1397-1475). Florentine School _____ 200

410. The Annunciation. *Master of the Louvre Predella* (Active c.1450). Venetian School _____ 152

NUMBER		PAGE

411. Madonna and Child. *Lorenzo Veneziano* (Dated works 1356-1372). Venetian School — 137

412. The Crucifixion. *Barnaba da Modena* (Active 1361-1383). Modenese School — 61

413. Madonna and Child with Angels. *Master of the Jarves Cassoni* (Active c.1450). Florentine School — 151

414. St. Sebastian. *Amico Aspertini* (c.1474-1552). Ferrarese-Bolognese School — 59

415. The Meeting of Dido and Aeneas. *Francesco di Giorgio* (1439-1502). Sienese School — 104

416. Madonna and Child with the Infant St. John. *Sodoma* (1477-1549). Sienese School — 190

417. The Holy Family. *Francesco Granacci* (1469-1543). Florentine School — 123

418. The Crucifixion with the Four Holy Women. *Giannicola di Paolo* (c.1460-1544). Umbrian School — 112

419. Portrait of a Gentleman. *Cariani* (Mentioned 1509-1547). Venetian School — 80

420. Madonna and Child with Two Angels. *Gentile da Fabriano* (c.1360-1427). Umbrian School — 109

421. Madonna and Child. *Giovanni Boccati* (Mentioned 1445-1480). Umbrian School — 74

422. St. Jerome Reading. *Alvise Vivarini* (Active 1457-1503/1505). Venetian School — 206

423. The Crucifixion. *Follower of Giotto*, XIV Century. Florentine School — 116

424. The Seven Arts. *Domenico di Michelino* (1417-1491). Florentine School — 97

425. The Seven Virtues. *Domenico di Michelino* (1417-1491). Florentine School — 97

426. Madonna Adoring the Child. *Pintoricchio* (c.1454-1513). Umbrian School — 170

427. Madonna and Child. *Francesco di Antonio Banchi* (Mentioned 1415). Florentine School — 61

428. St. Bartholomew. *Pietro Perugino* (c.1445-1523). Umbrian School — 166

429. The Agony in the Garden. *Benvenuto di Giovanni* (1436-c.1518). Sienese School — 72

430. The Adoration of the Child. *Cosimo Rosselli* (1439-1507). Florentine School — 180

431. The Martyrdom of St. Apollonia. *Neri di Bicci* (1419-c.1491). Florentine School — 158

432. Madonna and Child. *Niccolò di Pietro Gerini* (Active 1368-1414). Florentine School — 159

433. Christ and the Samaritan Woman. *Vincenzo Catena* (c.1470-1531). Venetian School — 84

434. St. Clare. *Andrea Vanni* (c.1332-c.1414). Sienese School — 202

435. Madonna and Child. *Girolamo del Pacchia* (1477-c.1535). Sienese School — 161

436. Madonna and Child. *Borgognone* (Active 1480-1523). Lombard School — 75

437. Scenes from a Legend. *Francesco Granacci* (1469-1543). Florentine School — 122

438. St. Jerome. *Alvise Vivarini* (Active 1457-1503/1505). Venetian School — 206

439. St. John the Baptist. *Alvise Vivarini* (Active 1457-1503/1505). Venetian School — 206

440. Portrait of a Lady as the Magdalen. *Giampietrino* (Active early XVI Century). Milanese School — 112

441. The Crucifixion. *Ugolino Lorenzetti* (Active 1320-1335). Sienese School — 136

442. The Presentation in the Temple. *L'Ortolano* (c.1488-c.1524). Ferrarese School — 161

443. Apollo and Marsyas. Florentine School, XVI Century — 103

444. Three Saints. *Sodoma* (1477-1549). Sienese School — 190

445. Madonna and Child. *Giovanni Bellini* (c.1430-1516). Venetian School — 70

446. Portrait of a Young Woman. *Girolamo di Benvenuto* (1470-1524). Sienese School — 120

447. A Saint Reading. *Vittore Carpaccio* (c.1455-1523/1526). Venetian School — 82

448. Portrait of a Senator. *Giovanni Bellini* (c.1430-1516). Venetian School — 70

449. Madonna and Child with the Infant St. John. *Andrea del Sarto* (1486-1530). Florentine School — 55

450. Portrait of a Man. *Cosimo Tura* (c.1430-1495). Ferrarese School — 200

451. Madonna and Child. *Cosimo Rosselli* (1439-1507). Florentine School — 180

452. The Adoration of the Magi. *Giovanni Baronzio* (Works dated 1344 and 1345). School of Rimini — 62

453. Madonna and Child with Angels. *Luca di Tommè* (Active 1355-1389). Sienese School — 138

454. The Visitation with Two Saints. *Piero di Cosimo* (1462-c.1521). Florentine School — 167

455. The Nativity. *Bernardino Luini* (c.1480-1532). Milanese School — 140

456. The Adoration of the Child with Saints and Donors. *Giovanni Battista Utili* (Mentioned 1498-1515). Florentine School — 202

457. Madonna and Child Enthroned with Saints. *Bernardo Daddi* (Mentioned 1312/1320 - c.1348). Florentine School — 94

NUMBER		PAGE
458.	Timocleia and the Thracian Commander. *Giovanni Battista Tiepolo* (1696-1770). Venetian School	193
459.	Madonna and Child with Four Saints. *Guariento* (Active 1338-1368/1370). Paduan School	125
460.	Madonna and Child. *Vincenzo Foppa* (1427/1430-1515/1516). Lombard School	103
461.	The Crucifixion with Madonna and Saints. *Lorenzo di Niccolò* (Mentioned 1392-1411). Florentine School	137
462.	Saint Luke the Evangelist. *Giovanni di Paolo* (1403-1482). Sienese School	119
463.	Madonna and Child. *Giacomo Pacchiarotto* (1474-c.1540). Sienese School	161
464.	The Nativity with the Infant St. John. *Piero di Cosimo* (1462-c.1521). Florentine School	168
465.	Madonna and Child. *Girolamo Romanino* (Active 1510-1562). Brescian School	180
466.	St. Catherine. *Pietro degli Ingannati* (Mentioned 1529-1548). Venetian School	125
467.	The Creation of Eve. *Fra Bartolommeo* (1472-1517). Florentine School	63
468.	St. Margaret. Sienese School (*Niccolò di Segna?*) c.1330	188
469.	The Annunciation. *Girolamo da Santa Croce* (Active 1503-1556). Venetian School	184
470.	The Holy Family with Saints. *Fra Bartolommeo* (1472-1517) and *Fra Paolino* (c.1490-1547). Florentine School	63
471.	St. Christopher. *Giovanni Antonio Pordenone* (c.1483-1539). Venetian School	172
472.	Madonna and Child. *Franciabigio* (c.1482-1525). Florentine School	105
473.	The Meditation of St. Jerome. *Garofalo* (1481-1559). Ferrarese School	108
474.	Minerva at the Forge of Vulcan. *Paris Bordone* (1500-1571). Venetian School	75
475.	The Assumption of the Virgin. *Girolamo da Carpi* (1501-1556). Ferrarese School	121
476.	Landscape with Figures. *Alessandro Magnasco* (1667-1749). Genoese School	143
477.	St. Peter. *Vincenzo Civerchio* (1468/1470-c.1544). Lombard School	86
478.	The Entombment. *Giovanni Francesco Caroto* (c.1480-after 1555). School of Verona	80
479.	Madonna Enthroned with Two Saints. *Pellegrino di Mariano* (Active 1449-1492). Sienese School	163
480.	The Holy Family. *Pontormo* (1494-c.1556). Florentine School	171
481.	St. Lucretia. *Dosso Dossi* (c.1479-c.1542). Ferrarese School	99
482.	Seascape with Friars. *Alessandro Magnasco* (1667-1749). Genoese School	141
483.	The Adoration of the Magi. *Master of the Bambino Vispo* (Active c.1400-c.1430). Florentine School	150
484.	Madonna and Child. *Girolamo da Treviso* (c.1450-c.1496). Venetian School	121
485.	Madonna and Child. *Mariotto Albertinelli* (1474-1515). Florentine School	51
486.	The Annunciation. *Giovanni del Biondo* (Active 1356-1392). Florentine School	116

Mellon Collection, 1940

NUMBER		PAGE
487.	William Vans Murray. *Mather Brown* (1761-1831). American School	7
488.	The Washington Family. *Edward Savage* (1761-1817). American School	8
489.	Joseph Coolidge. *Gilbert Stuart* (1755-1828). American School	8
490.	Mrs. Richard Yates. *Gilbert Stuart* (1755-1828). American School	10
491.	Lawrence Yates. *Gilbert Stuart* (1755-1828). American School	8
492.	George Washington. *Gilbert Stuart* (1755-1828). American School	9
493.	John Randolph. *Chester Harding* (1792-1866). American School	7
494.	Alexander Hamilton. *John Trumbull* (1756-1843). American School	10
495.	John Randolph. *Gilbert Stuart* (1755-1828). American School	10
496.	Colonel Guy Johnson. *Benjamin West* (1738-1820). American School	10
497.	Richard, Earl Howe. *John Singleton Copley* (1738-1815). American School	7
498.	A Young Man in a Large Hat. *Frans Hals* (c.1580-1666). Dutch School	26
499.	A Turk. *Rembrandt Van Ryn* (1606-1669). Dutch School	31
500.	Portrait of a Flemish Lady. *Sir Anthony Van Dyck* (1599-1641). Flemish School	42
501.	The Maas at Dordrecht. *Aelbert Cuyp* (1620-1691). Dutch School	23

Kress Collection (Loans)

NUMBER		PAGE

502. Madonna and Child. *Verrocchio* (1435-1488). Florentine School — 205

503. Madonna and Child. *Giacomo Pacchiarotto* (1474-c.1540). Sienese School — 161

504. The Crucifixion. *Niccolò da Foligno* (c.1430-1502). Umbrian School — 159

505. St. Margaret. *Sassetta* (Active 1423-1450). Sienese School — 184

506. St. Apollonia. *Sassetta* (Active 1423-1450). Sienese School — 184

507. Scenes from the Life of the Virgin. *Guidoccio Cozzarelli* (Mentioned 1450-1499). Sienese School — 91

508. The Nativity with St. Jerome. *Girolamo di Benvenuto* (1470-1524). Sienese School — 120

509. Christ Washing the Feet of the Apostles. *Jacopo Bellini* (?) (c.1400-1470/1471). Venetian School — 71

510. Madonna and Child with Saints and the Crucifixion. *Contemporary of Duccio* (Active 1300-1320). Sienese School — 101

511. Madonna and Child with Donor. *Bernardo Daddi* (Mentioned 1312/1320-c.1348). Florentine School — 95

512. The Adoration of the Shepherds. *Pseudo-Boccaccino* (Beginning of XVI Century). Lombard School — 73

513. The Coronation of the Virgin. *Taddeo di Bartolo* (c.1362-1422). Sienese School — 191

514. Madonna and Child. *Lorenzo Monaco* (c.1370-c.1425). Florentine School — 136

515. Madonna and Child with Two Angels. *Francesco Granacci* (1469-1543). Florentine School — 123

516. St. John the Baptist. *Jacopo del Casentino* (Active 1339-1349/1358). Florentine School — 126

517. St. Lucy. *Jacopo del Casentino* (Active 1339-1349/1358). Florentine School — 126

518. St. John the Baptist and St. Sebastian. *Giovanni Boccati* (Mentioned 1445-1480). Umbrian School — 74

519. Madonna and Child Enthroned with Saints and Angels. *Bernardo Daddi* (Mentioned 1312/1320-c.1348). Florentine School — 95

NUMBER		PAGE

520. Madonna and Child with Angels. Italian School (Central) XIII Century — 125

521. St. Catherine of Alexandria. *Pietro Lorenzetti* (Active c.1305-c.1348). Sienese School — 135

522. The Nativity. *Paolo Fiamingo* (1540-1596). Flemish-Venetian School — 163

523. Ex Voto. *Gian Francesco de' Maineri* (Mentioned 1489-1504). Ferrarese School — 143

524. Madonna and Child. *Giovanni Antonio Boltraffio* (1467-1516). Milanese School — 74

525. Pietà. *Lo Spagna* (Active 1470-1528). Umbrian School — 190

526. St. John the Baptist. *Domenico Veneziano* (?) (c.1400-1461). Florentine School — 98

527. Madonna and Child with Saints. *Contemporary of Cimabue*, XIII Century. Florentine School — 86

528. The Baptism of Christ. *Alessandro Magnasco* (1667-1749). Genoese School — 142

529. The Holy Family with Angels. *Domenico Beccafumi* (1482/1486-1551). Sienese School — 66

530. Portrait of a Girl. *Giuseppe Maria Crespi* (1665-1747). School of Bologna — 92

531. Madonna and Child with Saints. *Simone dei Crocefissi* (Active 1355-after 1399). School of Bologna — 189

532. Christ Calling St. Peter. *Alessandro Magnasco* (1667-1749). Genoese School — 142

533. The Last Supper. *Sebastiano Ricci* (1659-1734). Venetian School — 176

534. Bindo Altoviti. *Raphael* (1483-1520). Umbrian School — 175

535. Madonna and Child. *Botticelli* (1444-1510). Florentine School — 77

536. The Annunciation. *Fra Filippo Lippi* (c.1406-1469). Florentine School — 132

537. The Coronation of the Virgin. *Filippino Lippi* (1457-1504). Florentine School — 130

538. Madonna and Child with Saints. *Giovanni Bellini* (c.1430-1516). Venetian School — 71

539. Madonna Enthroned with Saints and Angels. *Raffaele dei Carli* (c.1470-c.1525). Florentine School — 173

Additional Gifts, 1941-1942

NUMBER   PAGE   NUMBER   PAGE

545. Advice to a Young Artist. *Honoré Daumier*   548. Don Bartolomé Sureda. *Francisco José de Goya*
      (1808-1879). French School. Gift of Duncan   *y Lucientes* (1746-1828). Spanish School. Gift
      Phillips, 1941 _____ 46   of Mr. and Mrs. P. H. B. Frelinghuysen, in
                                                                          memory of her father and mother, Mr. and Mrs.
546. Madonna and Child with St. Mary Magdalen   H. O. Havemeyer, 1941 _____ 212
      and St. Catherine. *Pietro Lorenzetti* (Active
      c.1305-c.1348). Sienese School. In memory of
      Felix M. Warburg. Gift of his wife, 1941 _____ 135   549. Doña Teresa Sureda. *Francisco José de Goya*
                                                                          y Lucientes (1746-1828). Spanish School. Gift
547. A Dominican Preaching. *Domenico Morone*   of Mr. and Mrs. P. H. B. Frelinghuysen, in
      (c.1442-after 1517). School of Verona. In   memory of her father and mother, Mr. and Mrs.
      memory of Felix M. Warburg. Gift of his wife,   H. O. Havemeyer, 1941 _____ 213
      1941 _____ 156

LIST OF SCULPTURE

Mellon and Kress Collections

NUMBER   PAGE

A - 1. Madonna and Child. *Donatello* (c.1386-1466). Florentine School. Mellon Collection, 1937 _____ 228

A - 2. Bust of a Little Boy. *Desiderio da Settignano* (1428-1464). Florentine School. Mellon Collection, 1937 _____ 227

A - 3. Madonna and Child. *Desiderio da Settignano* (1428-1464). Florentine School. Mellon Collection, 1937 _____ 226

A - 4. The Young Christ with St. John the Baptist. *Desiderio da Settignano* (1428-1464). Florentine School. Mellon Collection, 1937 _____ 226

A - 5. Madonna and Child. *Agostino di Duccio* (1418-after 1480). Florentine School. Mellon Collection, 1937 _____ 223

A - 6. Charity. *Mino da Fiesole* (1431-1484). Florentine School. Mellon Collection, 1937 _____ 231

A - 7. Faith. *Mino da Fiesole* (1431-1484). Florentine School. Mellon Collection, 1937 _____ 231

A - 8. A Princess of the House of Aragon. *Francesco da Laurana* (c.1425-1502). Venetian School. Mellon Collection, 1937 _____ 230

A - 9. Lodovico Sforza, called Il Moro. *Giovanni Antonio Amadeo* (or *Omodeo*) (1447-1522). Lombard School. Mellon Collection, 1937 _____ 223

A-10. Gian Galeazzo Sforza. *Giovanni Antonio Amadeo* (or *Omodeo*) (1447-1522). Lombard School. Mellon Collection, 1937 _____ 223

A-11. Madonna and Child with Cherubim. *Andrea della Robbia, Atelier.* Florentine School. Mellon Collection, 1937 _____ 234

A-12. Madonna and Child with God the Father and Cherubim. *Andrea della Robbia, Atelier.* Florentine School. Mellon Collection, 1937 _____ 233

A-13. The Virgin in Adoration. *Andrea della Robbia* (1435-1525). Florentine School. Mellon Collection, 1937 _____ 233

A-14. Madonna and Child. *Antonio Rossellino* (1427-1478). Florentine School. Mellon Collection, 1937 _____ 235

NUMBER   PAGE

A-15. Madonna and Child. *Mino da Fiesole* (1431-1484). Florentine School. Mellon Collection, 1937 _____ 231

A-16. Giuliano de' Medici. *Verrocchio* (1435-1488). Florentine School. Mellon Collection, 1937 _____ 238

A-17. Putto Poised on a Globe. *Verrocchio* (1435-1488). Florentine School. Mellon Collection, 1937 _____ 237

A-18. Bust of a Lady. Florentine School, XV Century. Mellon Collection, 1937 _____ 227

A-19. Bust of St. John the Baptist. *Donatello* (c.1386-1466). Florentine School. Mellon Collection, 1937 _____ 227

A-20. Mercury. *Giovanni Bologna* (1524-1608). Flemish-Florentine School. Mellon Collection, 1937 _____ 229

A-21. Venus Anadyomene. *Jacopo Sansovino* (1486-1570). Florentine-Venetian School. Mellon Collection, 1937 _____ 236

A-22. Bacchus and a Young Faun. *Jacopo Sansovino* (1486 - 1570). Florentine - Venetian School. Mellon Collection, 1937 _____ 236

A-23. The Adoration of the Shepherds. *Annibale Fontana* (1540-1587). Lombard School. Kress Collection, 1939 _____ 228

A-24. Kneeling Angel. *Giovanni Antonio Amadeo* (or *Omodeo*) (1447-1522). Lombard School. Kress Collection, 1939 _____ 224

A-25. Kneeling Angel. *Giovanni Antonio Amadeo* (or *Omodeo*) (1447-1522). Lombard School. Kress Collection, 1939 _____ 224

A-26. Madonna and Child. *Giovanni Antonio Amadeo* (or *Omodeo*) (1447-1522). Lombard School. Kress Collection, 1939 _____ 223

A-28. Madonna and Child. *Francesco di Simone Ferrucci* (1437-1493). Florentine School. Kress Collection, 1939 _____ 228

A-30. Bust of a Lady (Isotta da Rimini?). *Desiderio da Settignano* (1428-1464). Florentine School. Kress Collection, 1939 _____ 227

NUMBER | PAGE

A-31. Madonna and Child. *Antonio Rossellino* (1427-1478). Florentine School. Kress Collection, 1939 _____ 235

A-32. The Nativity. *Domenico Gagini* (Mentioned 1448-1492). Lombard School. Kress Collection, 1939 _____ 230

A-33. St. Peter. *Andrea della Robbia* (1435-1525). Florentine School. Kress Collection, 1939 _____ 234

A-34. Madonna and Child. *Luca della Robbia* (1400-1482). Florentine School. Kress Collection, 1939 _____ 234

A-35. Bust of the Christ Child. *Andrea della Robbia* (1435-1525). Florentine School. Kress Collection, 1939 _____ 233

A-36. Bust of St. John the Baptist. *Andrea della Robbia* (1435-1525). Florentine School. Kress Collection, 1939 _____ 233

A-37. The Adoration of the Shepherds. *Verrocchio* (1435-1488). Florentine School. Kress Collection, 1939 _____ 238

A-38. Madonna and Child. *Master of the Marble Madonnas* (Active c.1845-c.1515). Florentine School. Kress Collection, 1939 _____ 231

A-39. Madonna and Child. *Tino di Camaino* (Mentioned 1312-1337). Tuscan School. Kress Collection, 1939 _____ 236

A-40 Madonna and Child with Saints. *Pyrgoteles* (Mentioned 1513-1531). Venetian School. Kress Collection, 1939 _____ 232

NUMBER | PAGE

A-41. Cherubs Playing with a Swan. *Jean Baptiste Tubi* (1630/1636 - 1700). Italo-French School. Mellon Collection, 1940 _____ 219

A-42. Cherubs Playing with a Lyre. *Pierre Legros* (1629-1714). French School. Mellon Collection, 1940 _____ 219

A-43. Monumental Urn. *Clodion* (1738-1814). French School. Mellon Collection, 1940 _____ 219

A-44. Monumental Urn. *Clodion* (1738-1814). French School. Mellon Collection, 1940 _____ 219

KRESS COLLECTION (LOANS)

A-45. Pietà. *Giovanni della Robbia* (1469-1529/1530). Florentine School _____ 235

A-46. St. Catherine of Siena. *Mino da Fiesole* (1431-1484). Florentine School _____ 232

A-47. A Singing Angel. *Pietro Lombardo* (c.1435-1515). Lombard-Venetian School _____ 230

A-48. Bust of the Young Christ. *Giovanni della Robbia* (1469-1529/1530). Florentine School 234

A-49. Bust of a Warrior. *Antonio Pollaiuolo* (1432-1498). Florentine School _____ 232

A-50. Bust of a Florentine Statesman. *Benedetto da Maiano* (c.1442-1497). Florentine School _____ 224

A-51. St. Sebastian. *Matteo Civitale* (1436-1501). Tuscan School _____ 226

A-62. Louis XIV. *Lorenzo Bernini* (1598-1680). Italian School _____ 225